CHILDHOOD REGAINED

BOOKS BY THE SAME AUTHOR

L'enfance gagnée (French)

Balance (English)

The Spider's Web (English)

Les trésors cachés (French)

*The King and the Widow
One Thousand and One Camels* (English)

Saadani & le prince (French)

EMILE TUBIANA

CHILDHOOD REGAINED

A ten-year-old boy's WWII memories

LPI

L'enfance gagnée was first published in
French, in Germany in 1977.

Initial translation 1986.
Present second edition of
L'enfance gagnée in English includes
the author's 2010-2011 revisions and edits.

*Cover and book design:
Viviane Tubiana*

LPI

Copyright 2011, 2020 by Emile Tubiana
All rights reserved. No part of this book may be reproduced,
scanned, or distributed in any printed or electronic form
without permission.

First Edition: January 2011
Second Edition: August 2020
Printed in the United States of America
ISBN: 0-9914488-3-9
ISBN-13: 978-0-9914488-3-8

CHILDHOOD REGAINED

To all the children of the world

EMILE TUBIANA

CONTENTS

Preface 11
Historical Sketch of My Hometown 15
My Town (Poem) 20
Beautiful Child I (Poem) 22
Beautiful Child II (Poem) 24
Memories (Poem) 26
Dreaming in Paris 29
School Friends 43
Sunday on the Seine River 57
My Hometown 61
My Father's Flowers 71
The Day Our School Closed 77
Facts 81
The Day Bombing Started 83
Assessing the Damage in Our Street 113
Our Desperate Search for a Safe Place 121
The Club of the Fearful 133
Necessity (Poem) 143
On the Nezer Farm 145
The Front Line Is Coming Closer 153
Fleeing to Nowhere 157
On the Train 165

CHILDHOOD REGAINED

Typhus 173
Returning to Our Town 187
"Their Name Liveth For Evermore" 202
The Liberated Zones 205
Back to School 217
The End of the American Presence 225
Postwar Summer Vacation 231
Life Goes On 235
The Conscription of Tunisian Peasants....245
Destiny (Poem) 251
Feelings (Poem) 252
Which Way to Go (Poem) 254
Spiritual Lift (Poem) 256
Their Moral Values (Poem).......................258
Hope (Poem) 259
The Gem (Poem).......................................259
Gifts of Life (Poem)..................................260

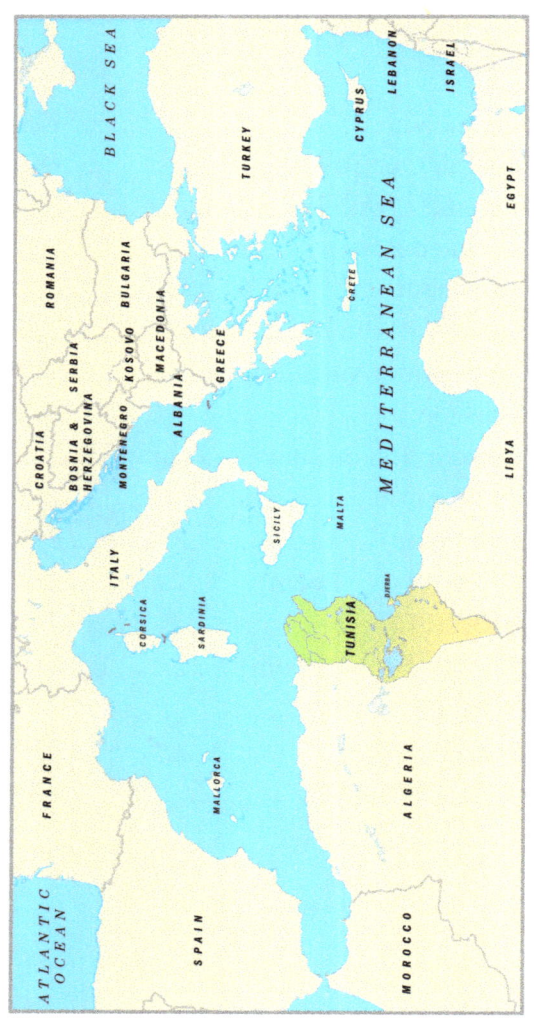

Tunisia and the Mediterranean Sea

PREFACE

In 1943-1944, when the frontline of WWII moved to Sicily, I started taking notes about some facts which impacted my family. As there were no notebooks available, I wrote my notes on any piece of paper I could put my hands on, such as the inside of cigarette packs that soldiers had discarded. Later, I continued writing my recollections and my impressions on sheets of paper, which I kept in a bag. Those papers are now in a folder in one of my drawers.

I wrote this book to preserve the memories of my time, my family, my town and its people for my children, my grandchildren and the coming generations, as well as for the descendants of the people of my town and for all my readers.

When I started writing this book I first

had to dive into a world distant in time and yet so close to me that it had become a part of my very being. This world awakened in me an avalanche of friendly and pleasant feelings. I felt that I was infused with the same powerful stream that filled my entire being when I was eight years old. I wanted to hold on to this feeling. I avoided any thoughts or actions which could have cut short this lovely, invisible, and beautiful stream.

I thought about the people who had been sheltered in the old houses for generations in the neighborhood where I was born. This thought came to me like a well-known perfume. Many faces of family members and of other people of my town appeared to me one after the other as if to say, "We know you."

I couldn't remember any names, but they seemed very close to me, as if we were one big family. This way I understood that the bond with the land and its inhabitants plays a great role in our life. While remembering them, I felt a pleasant and strong vibration which passed through my entire body like a friendly current.

I can clearly say that I love the land and its inhabitants as they are. I am confident that the people of Béja will always be in my heart like the seeds of wheat, which for centuries have made that land famous and rich.

EMILE TUBIANA

PHOTO BY EMILE SULTAN

View of Béja

HISTORICAL SKETCH OF MY HOMETOWN

Sixty-two miles from Tunis, between the Medjerdah River and the Mediterranean Sea, against the foothills of the Khroumire, the city of Béja softly spreads its white terraces and red roofs dominated by the imposing ruins of the old Roman fortress on the sides of Djebel Acheb, facing the greening meadows.

Whether you approach the city from the mountains by way of Souk el Khemis or from the sea by way of Tunis or Tabarka, you cannot miss the spectacular view that surprises and enchants every visitor.

The origin of Béja is lost in the beginnings of time. Famous for its fertile soil, it attracted all the masters of the Mediterranean coast. The Phoenicians set up important trading posts. Their presence is found through numerous Punic necropolises that have recently been unearthed. The Carthaginians, recognizing the importance of maintaining their authority in this area, built a garrison and fortified the city.

Béja was extremely desirable, not only because of its fertile soil but also because of its geographic location. It was at the doorway of a mountain range and at the intersection of the roads from Carthage and Tunis, going toward Cirta and Hippone. On several occasions it was assaulted, brutally burned, and destroyed either by the Carthaginians, the Numidians, the Romans, or, later on, by the Vandals. The Numidian king Jugurtha established the headquarters of his government in the city.

Originally the city was named Waga, which became Vacca and then Vaga under the Romans and eventually Badja under the Arabs.

The Romans dismantled the old

Carthaginian citadel and replaced it with a new one; they built fortifications that are still standing today. Under the Roman domination, Béja became prosperous and was the center of a diocese. According to Salluste, who relates the details of the famous war between Jugurtha and Metellus for the possession of Béja, the town was the wealthiest warehouse of the kingdom and an important center of commerce.

Taken and destroyed by the Vandals, its citadel and ramparts were demolished, and the abandoned city remained in that state for a century until the arrival of the Byzantines. They renovated the fortress and took real pleasure in beautifying the city.

Beginning with the seventh century, Béja was under Arab and later under Turkish domination.

In 1880 France occupied Tunisia. On April 24, 1881 Béja was occupied by the troops of General Logerot who had arrived from Algeria through Le Kef.

To this day, Béja remains a picturesque city with wide horizons, a healthy climate, and rich and fertile soil. Another distinctive feature is its family life, its traditional friendliness and hospitality towards foreigners. *(Excerpt from the French brochure written by Father Neu, former priest of Béja.)*

The old church of Béja, built in 1898

CHILDHOOD REGAINED

In 1942, after a long period of calm and tranquility, Béja was furiously bombed by German airplanes, because of its key position leading to the roads of Tabarka, Bizerte and Algeria. The city became the stage for ferocious battles between the Germans and the Allies who fiercely defended it, at the expense of severe military and civilian losses. The Allies succeeded in stopping the Germans three miles from the entrance to Béja.

MY TOWN

Sweet ancestral shelter
Many a time besieged
Your ramparts were ravaged
But decimated evil seeds

In your immense greatness
Challenging the universe
Your wintery whiteness
Enhances your beauty

Your vast wheat fields
Your carpets of poppies
Have repeated in an echo
My joy, on summer eves

You guarded the childhood
Of my humble spirit
And it was to my advantage
That you fulfilled my destiny

CHILDHOOD REGAINED

You are a source of life
Without you my heart sinks
Into the shadow
Of an infinite world

You have directed my path
And the way to dawn
You are still guiding me
Towards tomorrow's life

You will be forever
Alive in my heart
Citadel of happiness
And valley of love

BEAUTIFUL CHILD I

Oh sweet and pure one, full of cheer and joy
Shine, twinkle, like the summer sun
Show your greatness, your glory,
   your wonder

Rise! Break through the night and
   the fog!
Your existence is not mere chance
Among children, grown-ups and
   the elderly

You know neither space nor time
Where you are it's always spring
That's why I have been waiting for you
   ever since

Let us walk towards you, towards your light
From the bottom of our hearts like from
   a quarry
Our songs and our prayers resound

CHILDHOOD REGAINED

Here you are in the firmament
Oh you! Beautiful child
As shiny as a diamond

You do not know melancholy, sadness,
Sorrow, fear, distress
Hatred, rancor or weakness...

You overcame my distrust
From my early childhood on
This is why I am confident

You discern our thoughts with astuteness
You penetrate the hearts that are ready
To live in love and peace

You act only your way
Without arrogance, pride or appearance
In the rhythm of your good pace

You know neither battle nor war
All men are brothers to you
In your life, that of your father

BEAUTIFUL CHILD II

You don't know intrigues or lies
Rancor, wrong or vengeance
With you all bad dreams vanish
You are my glory, my love and my good
    fortune

You are thinner than a needle
Your rays have no distance
In the dark you shine, you shine
To find you again, to keep you,
    what luck!

You appear as a lightning
Under the sun, the rain and the wind
Oh! You, my beautiful one!
    Oh! You, my dear one!
You do not know gold or silver

Our bodies are thrilled to feel you
In the deepest moments
You appear as a girl
Full of charm and sweetness

CHILDHOOD REGAINED

Thank you so very much for having come
From afar I recognized you
You are always welcome
You have been mine for a long time

MEMORIES

Numerous are those who think,
   forever lost
The truth of their childhood
   that time has tossed
It does not matter;
   daily life gives us bits of truth
That help us find
   what we lost from our youth.

We forget a friend's face,
   life provides new faces
The atmosphere differs,
   as we are in new places.
Today we speak of our past,
   tomorrow of today.
Each day has its truth;
   new events come into play

CHILDHOOD REGAINED

Each moment brings out
   some of our innermost
A banal event, sounds of rain,
   or wind on the coast
Bring out nostalgia, melancholy,
   sadness or longing,
Which are states of truth,
   of grace, or of belonging

Those with no feelings miss the truth,
   which is shy
At times when we cry
   and we can't explain why,
We cry for our youth,
   a beloved one, or our good
Many years later
   the reason will be understood.

EMILE TUBIANA

The Metro entrance at Place des Abbesses and the Sacré Coeur Basilica in Montmartre, Paris

DREAMING IN PARIS

It was nine o'clock in the morning when the church bells rang on Place des Abbesses. I ran downstairs to have my breakfast at the corner café on rue Antoinette. The neighborhood was already stirring. Several boys late for school hurried along with their school bags on their backs. Indifferent, an old woman was selling newspapers at the entrance of the *Metro* (subway).

The café was half filled with customers. Some leaning on the counter, others seated, they were drinking coffee and chatting. At the back was an empty table that a couple had hurriedly left; on the slightly wrinkled tablecloth stood two empty cups. From the next room came the clinking of billiard balls. As soon as the waiter saw me, he rushed towards me, greeted me with a professional smile on his face and cleaned the table. He knew me well, since I was a regular. He changed the tablecloth and brought me my usual cup of coffee and two hot croissants.

After this frugal breakfast, I took special pleasure in smoking my first cigarette of the day. I enjoyed watching the passersby through the window. It was my favorite time of day, when I could let myself daydream without being interrupted, oblivious to the surrounding noises. Millions of thoughts raced through my head. Everything was still new to me since I had only recently moved from North Africa to Paris. I had never experienced such noisy and busy life. Nothing left me indifferent. And I was very happy, like all young people on their first visit to the City of Light. I had known this city only through books and stories. Paris, so often described to us in school; Paris, so often the object of reveries on the class bench; Paris was a unique symbol during my childhood. As I sat in the café, all kinds of images marched through my head: the kings of France, the Middle Ages, Charlemagne, Joan of Arc, the Revolution, Napoleon, Dreyfus, Emile Zola, Maréchal Philippe Pétain, General De Gaulle, German soldiers, American soldiers, and the first British parachutists. In a sense, nothing was unknown to me. And yet, I felt removed from all of this, everything felt strange. This is how I understood that every human being is alone with himself.

I was finishing my second cup of coffee when Roland, a childhood friend, walked in. His curly hair was combed more carefully than usual. He was wearing a brown striped suit and had grown a mustache to look more mature. He had moved to Paris long before I had. Occasionally he would come and meet me in this café. We enjoyed reliving old times. Although he had some relatives in Paris he felt as out of place as I did. That day he looked as if he had some good news. He eagerly shared with me the arrival of our friend Vincent. I was delighted to hear about it. "He has just landed in town."

Another lost soul, I said to myself, but in fact I was happy to see my former classmates. Vincent was a devil in school. His parents were Italian. He had come to Paris on his own, they had preferred Italy. Paris appealed to him since most of his friends had settled there.

Would I recognize Vincent? I remembered how skinny he had been in school. He used to play center forward on our soccer team. He always knew his lessons perfectly, and of course, our teacher was very fond of him. I was trying to recapture the features of his face, but no luck. *I'll never recall that face*, I thought; it's disheartening; I can't remember him at all. Except for his blue eyes, I drew a blank. I blamed myself for having such a poor memory; why couldn't I even remember the shape of his face? After all, we had spent quite some time together. We once had a fight over a girl who actually didn't care for either one of us, but since she loved the attention of any boy, she flirted with both of us. Where could she be now? She was probably married. She was certainly not made for celibacy.

Roland and I exchanged a host of memories of a world which seemed far away. Our old friends from school were scattered all over. We had run into some of them by chance and knew what they were up to now, but most had disappeared from our lives forever. Many things had occurred since. We lived in different worlds. Our new occupations and our busy lives had disrupted our wishes, not leaving us much time to see each other as we would have liked to. The same was true for family members. However, we needed each other very badly in order to function well in this complicated and difficult world where circumstances had separated us.

Outside it started raining lightly. Roland, moved by the recollection of our memories, did not stop talking about school, our teacher, soccer, the priest, the rabbi and the days when we played hooky. I remember one morning when Vincent and I were deliberately late for school because we had stayed up late the night before playing around and had neglected to learn our lesson by heart. We thought that coming late would spare us the embarrassment of not being prepared when asked to recite the lesson, but as luck would have it, the assistant principal caught us sneaking in and told us to bring a note from our parents explaining why we were late. But the weather was so great that we had decided to play in the woods behind the school. However, in the evening a sense of remorse overwhelmed me and the lesson I had to memorize loomed over me. What should I choose? To miss school or to memorize those lines? I was torn between freedom and obedience. At home my father was looking at me with suspicion, which gave me the feeling he could read my thoughts. I guess my face gave me away. To save face, I took my book and started to learn my lesson by heart. And that note of apology I had to hand in the following day! How would I get it? My father would certainly not understand and I was risking a reprimand. Tired and worried I fell asleep.

I was no longer listening to Roland. He had succeeded in taking me way back into the past. He finally realized I was not with him. He got up and said, "See you tonight at my place, Vincent will be there."

Outside, the rain had gone from a drizzle to a downpour. As I crossed the street, I became soaked to the bone. Ah! My poor grandmother would have been unhappy to see me in this state. She resented my mother letting me go to school on cold and wet days. "What more are you going to learn? You are better off staying warm with me at home," she would say with her soft and caressing voice. "What's the point of arriving at school soaking wet; the two of us aren't going to get bored, are we?" I would look at her gratefully, already seeing myself saved from the martyrdom of school. I did not see any harm in it and was happy to stay with her and benefit from her warm presence. I thought of the birds that don't leave the nest until they are ready to fly. My grandmother had never gone to school, but she knew how to give us love and affection, which was much more enticing to me than the alphabet or the numbers. What is the good of going to school if it is not appealing? We have our whole life ahead of us to learn. Once our childhood ends, it's over, we are thrown out of our paradise. We are educated without regard to our inherent abilities and desires. And so we risk being put in a lifeless mold. What means do we have at that age to resist that life discipline imposed on us? We are helpless, but our case is not unique. The lion, for example, is also tamed against his will; consequently he loses his freedom and his crown when put behind the bars of a circus cage.

Our poor kindergarten teacher! She loved school so much that she never married. She had never known the feeling of motherhood. Her life was not easy with us, but she was always so understanding, even when we left live grasshoppers on her desk; all she would say was, "Oh! The poor little creatures!" We did not really intend to frighten her but it would amuse us to see her shudder. The next day we would bring her flowers to win her forgiveness, as we were really very fond of her. We enjoyed the grasshoppers, the birds, the flowers, we didn't see any harm in that, and it was all natural. She would say to us, "You are little devils, my children, but I love you because you are good-hearted." We spent our days either in class or outside in the covered playground. We built sandcastles. It was in this playground that we learned our first folk songs, *"Au clair de la lune,"* and *"Sur le pont d'Avignon."* We had no idea of the significance of "Avignon" then, but this way our teacher introduced us to French culture and to France. Yet, this was very far from our thoughts and our little sheltered environment.

At the end of the school day, the bell would ring and we would leave our castles and return to the world of the grownups, as our parents were waiting outside. We were too young to know the way to our own homes. When we would grow up, we would do the same for our children. After all, we, as children, lived in a different world and our parents could not penetrate the world of the little ones without our help. We had to learn our parents' language in order to express ourselves. We knew what we wanted, but the grownups could not understand us. We were in the same situation as foreigners who have to learn the customs and the language of the country in which they settle. Being children, whether we were Christians, Muslims or Jews, we spoke the same language, we understood each other. What bonded us together the most was the fact that we were of the same age.

For us, graduation to first grade meant that we were growing up, and with it, our understanding of grownups improved. Gradually, we discovered the world of the alphabet and the numbers. We learned them by heart, but we were not sure of their purpose. One thing we understood was that we were at the threshold of the complicated adult world which would perhaps lead us on unknown paths.

At school, our teachers didn't have the answers to our questions. They would stay vague or use words like "sin", "forbidden", "prohibited", and "not allowed" in their daily vocabulary, which seemed strange to us. No explanations were forthcoming; their meaning was left for us to guess.

The rules of the grownups were difficult to understand; nevertheless we understood them from our own angle. *When we grow up, we would follow these rules and perhaps we would create new ones*, I thought. Any rule we would adopt would probably not be right, since one must first know the limits of the meaning of good and evil as to find the right measure. Good is subjective, acceptable to some, not to others—similarly evil.

Today, spaceships go to the moon and tomorrow they may explore another planet. But a fact remains: we will discover the Moon or Mars without having discovered our own heart or that of our neighbor. Children do not need boats or spaceships to explore their world, for theirs is not so remote. Each of us can explore their world but to do so, we must forget we are adults. It is not easy to become a child again but it is the only way to enter their pure world and it is easier than we may think. After all, there is no need for a passport, money, education or baggage. It is so simple: just think plainly without malice or intrigue. We must free ourselves from the burdens that we carry along. We must be true to ourselves and recognize our own value, for in the children's world the roles are distributed without concern for hierarchy. All that matters is to be part of the game.

Class photo, Béja, 1939

SCHOOL FRIENDS

That evening I went to Roland's. There was a crowd. He had pleasantly surprised us, by inviting all our classmates who were in Paris. All were happy and welcomed each newcomer with exuberant joy. I was overwhelmed by the feeling which united us intimately and of which we were all aware. At first, I couldn't put a name to each face, it was total confusion.

Victor who was the last to leave Tunisia was able to recognize everyone without hesitation. He introduced each of them to me, saying, "Guess! Who is this? Do you remember Mr. Taboul, the grocer? And his son Jacques? Do you remember? Well, that's him!" This scene repeated itself many times. We would then hug each other like brothers who haven't seen each other for years.

After he greeted all the friends present, Roland came over to me leading a friend by the hand. "Here is one of our best childhood friends." I must confess that I did not recognize this young man. But Roland announced, "Our friend Vincent!" I jumped and kissed him. His face had changed and he had grown taller, his physique was imposing. The only thing unchanged was the color of his eyes. When I hugged him, there was no reciprocal emotion and I had the feeling that I had embraced a stranger. Nevertheless, he seemed moved and we rejoiced to see each other again. Our talk went late into the night. Before leaving, we made arrangements to meet the following morning.

The next morning, coming out of my place, I crossed rue des Abbesses, where street vendors had set up their fruit and vegetable stands on the sidewalks, drawing numerous shoppers, blocking the way of passersby. The drivers sounded their horns profusely. All this noise and commotion contributed to create the customary animation of populated neighborhoods. It was already ten o'clock. I tried to hurry by working my way through the crowd. I managed to edge myself through to the café La Tasse on the corner of rue Coulaincourt. Vincent was not there yet. He showed up later dressed in an old double-breasted coat as I was ordering *lait grenadine*, a pomegranate milkshake.

"I had a rough time finding my way around in the *Metro*," he said.

"You should have come on a horse," I replied.

"That's all I needed, with such traffic!"

"After just a few days in Paris you dared to come by *Metro*. Congratulations! I remember how difficult it was for me. It took me a long time to understand how the *Metro* system worked, and frankly, during my first days I avoided going out alone."

Vincent, who appeared embarrassed

for arriving late, listened to me carefully and seemed reassured. He said, "Have you been here for long?"

"No!" I answered, "Just a few minutes". He visibly relaxed and we started talking about the previous evening.

Then he became nervous and said, "I have problems with my Italian papers. And what is so strange is that I can't even speak Italian. In fact, I feel more French than Italian. Yesterday I went to the Police Headquarters and after the usual long wait, the clerk asked for my passport and demanded my reasons for coming to France saying, 'We've got enough French *pieds noirs* (literally 'black feet'; French North Africans), and, lo and behold! Now there are Italian *pieds noirs* arriving! That's too much.' To excuse myself I told him that I could not speak Italian and that at school we learned French, to which he replied, 'If we had to accept all those who learned French, we would not have any space left in France.' This led me to say,

'France is big enough and it is good for a country to be well populated.' My response didn't seem to satisfy him, he dismissed me by saying 'Come back tomorrow.' " Vincent told me about this first encounter with the immigration official in a rather discouraged tone. Then he asked me, "What does *pieds noirs* mean?"

"They are the *'bicots'*; this is a derogatory expression for the underprivileged of our society," I explained to Vincent. "In Tunisia we were known as 'Europeans', here we are *'pieds noirs'* or *'bicots'* if you prefer. Don't worry over such a trivial thing. All societies need scapegoats. Sometimes it's the Jews, in the coal mines it's the Polish. In America, it's the 'African-Americans' to quote Americans who want to refer to Blacks; in Germany, it's the *'Ausländer'*, in Israel, the '*Frenks*' or Ashkenazim, in Arab countries, depending on the situation it's the Copts, the Shiites or Sunnis, in Switzerland it's the *'Zozets'* and somewhere else the *'Chleux'*. You've got to get used to it, my dear friend."

"Yes, but at home it was…"

"It was what?"

"Well! We got along well!"

"Of course! Because we knew everyone. And don't forget we were born in the same city. Moreover, we were all immigrants, even the Arabs! You'll see, once you are settled, the area will become familiar to you and neighbors will know you, you and your fellow *'pied noirs'*. One must admit that Paris has its own phobias, even French people from the provinces are not really welcome here; they are called 'peasants'."

Somewhat reassured, Vincent asked me, "And what about my passport? In fact it is the first time I have had a passport. In Tunisia we did not need one."

"Yes, it's true, but we had other needs. For example we could not go from one place to another without a carriage. Well, let's talk about something else.

What would you like to order? A coffee and a croissant? I can't offer you *beignets* (doughnuts) or Tunisian couscous, for that we must go to Belleville."

"A coffee and a croissant will do."

To me, Vincent seemed to be like an angel who had come straight from heaven. He tried to appear calm and confident but his blue eyes betrayed him. From the look of his eyes, still innocent, I could see that he was filled with fear and anxiety. He looked at everything and everyone with the curiosity of a baby who starts looking at the world around him with wonder. I tried to talk about the beauty of Europe, and France in particular, but the talk always went back to Tunisia and to our childhood. He was still living in the past and to please him I played his game.

"Vincent, do you remember our teacher? And do you remember how one day we stayed away from school because of …"

He completed the sentence, "… of the

fable of the plowman and his children."

"Do you see the application of this fable's moral in today's world? Well, one can express it in these words, 'do not sell the legacy that your parents left you.' "

"Yes, but what's the good of all this when all our possessions, my future heritage, have been confiscated without our being able to protest?"

"You are such a materialist! Remember what our parents gave us morally; it is a legacy from which we benefit even during their lifetime and which cannot be taken away from us. And that's important. We possess our own treasures of immeasurable worth; for example, you, Vincent, were excellent at writing."

"So what?"

"Well, you can write, express yourself."

"Yes and then…"

"Well, you could write a book."

"On what?"

"Well, Vincent, on anything, why not on our town, or on our childhood for example."

"Even if I lack imagination?"

"You don't need imagination. All you have to do is simply write the truth about our childhood or about the war; write, write, simply write, I beg you."

Vincent carefully lit a cigarette and said, "Our childhood or the war! Who could possibly be interested in that?"

"You must be joking! I for one, plus all our friends and all our countrymen! If you'd like, I will help you; I will remind you of the facts, of the anecdotes, I will refresh your memory. All you will have to do is to let your pen guide you."

"Well, that sounds wonderful! And what a way to relive our childhood!"

"You see! And you'll be forced to talk about our town although you are miles away. Don't you understand that the place where we are becomes irrelevant and of no importance at all?"

"It's true! But you will have to devote much of your time to this task."

"Are you trying to tell me that you do not want my company?" At these words Vincent protested strongly, "Of course not, I would love to have your assistance and that would help me detach myself from this European society."

"Don't fool yourself, you won't escape the society; wherever you may be, society will be too." I noticed that even the thought of it scared him, so I continued to encourage him further. "You will need society to appreciate your talent and to make you known in the world."

After a little pause, he went back to his previous thoughts and asked, "And my Italian passport? What will become of it in all of this?"

"Forget about your passport for a moment, you don't need to worry about it. You'll see, you will begin to feel like you are in our town here!"

He smiled, and it was obvious he

was beginning to like his future role. The church clock struck noon as a group of teenagers walked into the café to get sandwiches for lunch. Vincent watched them, and told me, "Oh, these kids! They know nothing about our problems. They grew up in the same city where they lived when they were young, just like us, before we left our town. But now we are uprooted, overwhelmed with passport stories and *'pieds noirs'* stories as if it were our fault to have been born there, and to top it all, I from Italian parents and you from Jewish ones."

"Put these problems aside, there are more serious problems than that. What should the people of different skin color say? They think and feel like us, the only difference between them and us is that we are born from white parents; don't you see that their life among the white race is more difficult than ours? What are we doing to help them? Nothing, absolutely nothing.

My dear Vincent, feel content with

your life. This last war has disrupted the whole world. Entire populations have been displaced. The world is spinning faster and faster. Soon we'll see Americans in Russia, Arabs in America, and in Europe, etc. A strange mixture will be created. Soon we will see a second Tower of Babel. Villages will be transformed into huge cities with skyscrapers, while cities will be falling in ruins. And we call that progress! First, they created rights for men; now rights for women are a fact, and soon there will also be rights for children. Eventually we will have a quantity of rights. Maybe one day we will be able to define the meaning of 'men's duties', 'women's duties' and 'children's duties'. Don't worry, anyway everything will be computerized. Each of us will have a number; we'll be like robots."

"But this will be a catastrophe! What will we do with our feelings? Will it be the end of mankind?"

"Don't exaggerate; we haven't

reached that point yet. You and I must start doing something about it in order perhaps to change the course of development. It is not too late, but it is not too early either. Let's not waste any time. If only developing countries knew the price of progress! Listen, Vincent, it's getting late and I think it's time to go home. We'll see each other again towards the end of the week." I felt that it was enough for Vincent for one day, and knowing his difficulties with the subway, I decided to accompany him to his place. Vincent was happy and relieved to recognize his street.

EMILE TUBIANA

Conflans Sainte Honorine

SUNDAY ON THE SEINE RIVER

It was a Sunday in May, with a blue sky. Vincent and I had gone for a long walk along the Seine River, somewhat north of Conflans Sainte Honorine. Barges went up and down the river visually merging into the water. Vincent was ecstatic saying, "Nature is so beautiful! What tranquility! It's almost more beautiful than around our town."

"Come on, Vincent, every country, every nation has its beauty, it's just a matter of discovering it."

Children were walking along the water's edge, undulating from the passing barges. A fisherman with his rod was waiting patiently. But soon his line was pulled and an unfortunate fish tried desperately to free itself from the hook.

Its struggle for life seemed in vain. First disappointed with the size of his catch, the fisherman was suddenly overcome by a feeling of pity comparable to that of a king granting a pardon to a convict sentenced to death. "Poor little fish, you are too young to die", said the fisherman, and with a generous gesture and a wide spread arm, he threw it back into its own element.

The vignette was over and Vincent who had followed it closely said angrily, "This man has no heart! He has committed a crime by hurting this poor fish and throwing it back into the water without wondering what will become of it. It's unforgivable, one should …"

"What do you want to do? There is no law against this type of crime if it is a crime."

"What you are saying is absurd," answered Vincent overly sensitive.

"My dear Vincent, it would be asking too much from a fisherman to forbid him to act in this way, for this is his hobby. And if one had to create new laws they would deal with more important and more urgent issues. One should, one should…"

A cool northern wind bent the young blades of grass. The fisherman was getting impatient; the wind was against him but at the same time it saved the life of many fish lured by the bait. He cast his line again and again without luck. Vincent was thrilled by the fisherman's vain efforts. "Fortunately there are still natural forces which protect the well-being of creatures."

"You see," I added, "it's not always necessary for men to create laws. Mother Nature manages to protect her subjects, fortunately for us. She does not take into consideration our calculations. However, as soon as man finds himself away from society, he feels entitled to do everything he wants, but in many cases the forces of Nature put an end to harmful deeds."

Rue de la Gare, Béja

CHILDHOOD REGAINED

MY HOMETOWN

I remember my home. How much I loved it! How much I miss it now. To love one's home does not mean to love the stones with which the house has been built, but the real love stems from the atmosphere and the warmth created by its old rooms, the radiance of the people who live there, those who visit, and from the heirlooms and memories it contains.

I have left my entire childhood there. Today it is easy for me to remember that time. It is not difficult for me to relive this period, which was the sweetest and happiest time of my life. As a child, like everyone my age, I was eager to grow up; I was aware of the happy atmosphere surrounding me from all sides, of my family's affection enveloping me and even of the happiness emanating from my little person. It is only now that I am able to appreciate its true value. One always cherishes happy moments in retrospect and for this reason I have never wished to return to my native town. I was afraid not to find all that I left behind. Would the streets, my family home still be the same? Would they not seem to me like historical monuments? And my school, where I had spent my best years? What would I find? Surely a new town with an atmosphere entirely different from the one I once knew, with new and unfamiliar faces! Seeing my town again after so many years would give me the impression of seeing an old theater converted into a museum filled with tourists. What charm would it have without its real actors and its original décor?

Our memories? They are the real, true history of each of us. However, except for those who lived it, we are not able to feel the nature, the intensity and the depth of the emotions that emerge from it. Certainly, it is not easy for others to understand our truth. As I think of my parents' home, a different memory of my childhood comes to mind.

I am neither a religious fanatic nor do I want to preach the Jewish religion to others. What I am trying to describe here is, above all, the atmosphere which surrounded us, created by my parents. It was the way of life that our ancestors knew how to shape and to envelop us with. To give an example, every Thursday the women visited the cemetery and the tombs of members of the family and friends. They cleaned the marble tombstones, and then they placed sprays of flowers on them. Even among the wealthy, some women volunteered to clean the synagogue and light the oil lamps for those who left the community for the world of light. Never has anyone desecrated either our cemetery or our synagogue.

All inhabitants of the town respected each other, regardless of their religion or their ethnicity. After school, the girls assisted their mothers in cleaning the house and preparing the food for the Shabbat eve dinner and for the Shabbat day meals, as on Shabbat the Jews refrained from doing any work, as prescribed by Jewish law. After school, the boys went to Hebrew school, which was located within the building of the synagogue, to rehearse the songs for Friday night and for Shabbat. Some boys repeated the song of *Eshet Hayel* (Proverbs 31:10–31—A good wife who can find?) and others sang *Yegdal Elohim Hai* (A song of praise for the Living God) or rehearsed the *Parasha* (the weekly portion of the law) and the *Haftara* (the chapter from the Prophets) for Shabbat. Most Jewish women used to light oil lamps in memory of Rabbi Meir, of Rabbi Shimeon Bar Yohai, other saints of their choice, or recently departed family members. On Fridays, the women were busy from dawn to the lighting of the candles (before sundown) preparing the meals for Friday night and Shabbat day. My Muslim neighbors respected the Friday, as this was their religious day of the week. For our Christian neighbors, it was the Sunday. They wore their best clothes, preparing for Mass and for a festive meal afterwards, either at a restaurant or at home. We lived in good harmony among the different communities in our neighborhood.

Before my father came home, my mother set the table with a white tablecloth and our best china and cutlery. Our Friday night dinner was the traditional North African couscous with meat, vegetables, *boulettes* (fried and then cooked meatballs) and *osbana* (home-made sausage cooked in the soup, made of organ meat, a little rice, spinach, mint and spices). Then there were some of the traditional Shabbat day dishes, such as the *dfina*, either a meat and bean stew which was left to simmer on embers all night, or the *pkayla* (a fried spinach dish with meat, very special to that region), or *kamakh* (a stew of wheat and meat), or *nikitous* soup (chicken soup with tiny handmade pasta, rolled between the fingers, the size of a peppercorn, which the women prepared during the week). For Shabbat afternoon they prepared cold dishes, to avoid any work, such as roasted chicken eaten cold, a fish dish, a fruit dish, large omelets called *ma'akood*, made with cooked and fresh eggs, cooked meat, chicken or fish, and potatoes, green onions, pepper, and spices, sometimes mixed with other ingredients that varied from family to family, and which were finally baked in the oven. Another dish was the *maghmooma*, a vegetable stew made of fresh tomatoes, garlic, green and red peppers and spices, which was eaten cold. There were also all kinds of salads. And I cannot forget the various cakes and pastries and the bread, which my mother used to bake every single day. In our region, the women prepared a glass full of home squeezed grape juice for the prayer. The Arabs prepared the aromatic herbs called *rehan* for the Jews' prayer on all that smells good, at the end of Shabbat day.

When my father arrived home, all noise stopped. He usually brought with him the aromatic herbs, jasmine flowers or other flowers of the season. My mother used to send me around to the neighbors with portions of the dishes she had prepared to give them a taste of our cooking. At my age, it was great fun for me to visit our neighbors.

After school, we boys quickly washed up and put on our best clothes. Some said their prayers at home and some went to the synagogue. I used to accompany my father to the synagogue and sometimes I went to a more remote synagogue located in the Ayn Shemsh neighborhood, where only the older generation, who could no longer walk a lot, was congregating in a private house. For me, these visits and prayers were most memorable.

After services, when I came back home, I was happy and full of love. Our home was brightly lit and the two candles enhanced the beauty of the table, where my mother placed the bouquet of flowers in the center. This created a festive atmosphere. The two loaves of bread, covered by an embroidered napkin, were lying next to the flowers and the bottle of wine that my father used to bring with him. A serene ambiance was created and emanated also from the smiles of my mother and my five sisters, who prepared a very nice welcome for us. All of this gave me a feeling of divine love, happiness and joy, which stayed with me to this very day.

When I think about my family, I feel a constant spiritual stream flowing and inundating my soul and my entire being. This is what my parents' home means to me. I always thank my parents for giving us such a rich spiritual heritage. Without any university diplomas, through their way of life and everything they did, they instilled in us the respect and the love for others. With their simplicity and their natural sense of all that is sacred, regardless of their religious affiliation, they knew how to instill joy and to awaken the sacred soul in us.

EMILE TUBIANA

CHILDHOOD REGAINED

MY FATHER'S FLOWERS

I remember my first home, when I was three years old. It was a small apartment on the second floor with a lovely and spacious balcony. When my mother was busy in the kitchen she let me stay on the balcony watching the kids play in the street. I could see at least a few hundred yards away. On that balcony I sometimes played with my two older sisters. The eldest was seven years old and when my mother was away she was like a mother to us. The balcony was a great hobby place for my father. After work he used to grow carnations in flower boxes. His carnations were red, pink and white. Everyone who saw them admired them for their beauty.

He took care of them with so much love, precision, and devotion. He dealt meticulously with his flowers like a mother taking care of her baby. Many times I sat on the floor of the balcony for hours observing him and his flowers with patience. He was always doing something on that balcony. He was watering them every day, cleaning the balcony floor, sometimes clipping the wilted leaves, changing the potting soil, and when the stems were thick, strong and tall enough, he would start his enhancement operation like a surgeon.

My father took a tiny knife and with his left hand he held the stem of the carnation and measured the height. Then he made a small mark on the stem with his finger. Afterwards he made an incision with the knife, just enough to insert a grain of barley. Then he bound the stem with a small bandage made from leftover material from my mother's sewing. His job was then to water the plants and to take care of them. "No one should touch them," he said to my mother. Every day, when he came home from work he went straight to the balcony.

My mother used to tell us, "Do not touch Father's flowers." For us it was a fascinating experience to watch how the small stems were growing and making flowers. When the carnations had grown big enough, my father enjoyed watching them every day. We kids did too. One day my older sister, who loved my father very much, had a great idea. Wanting to help my father, she cut the carnations from their stems one by one and arranged them on the floor. She believed that he would be very pleased to see them that way.

When my mother realized what my sister had done, she was dumbstruck, as she didn't know what to say. The shock was too strong and we all awaited my father's arrival with emotion and apprehension. My sister didn't realize why we were so quiet, without a word of appreciation. She couldn't understand why no one gave her a compliment. When my father arrived, he went straight to the balcony, as usual.

When he saw his flowers lying on the floor like dead animals, he was shocked at first. He looked towards the street, to see if there was no one from the neighbors' children who could have done it. Then he entered the living room and looked at my mother in silence, but we all awaited an exclamation or a punishment. Then he looked left and right and my mother, who always taught us to tell the truth no matter what, looked at my father and said, "We have no bad neighbors in our area," then with a sweet voice she continued, "No outsider did this great job, only your lovely daughter Clémence." My father's face changed from tense to a smile and then he said, "Do I have a better flower than my lovely daughter?" My older sister smiled and gave my father a big hug.

CHILDHOOD REGAINED

*The balcony of our old house
was damaged during the war.*

EMILE TUBIANA

The schoolyard, Béja

THE DAY OUR SCHOOL CLOSED

It was the day when our principal told us that our school would close down. All the teachers were present, dressed in their Sunday best, like on exam days. They assembled us all and made us line up in the covered playground. There was total and complete silence. The music teacher came forward, as he would for a rehearsal, the grave expression on his face revealing a profound sadness. With a sweet and low, barely audible voice, he whispered, "Children, let us sing *la Marseillaise*" (the French national anthem). I felt he really had a hard time keeping up with us; it was difficult for him to hide his emotion.

Then the principal came over to us. We were struck by the pallor of his face, which confirmed the seriousness of the situation. With slow movements and in moving silence his eyes ran from one end of the playground to the other, photographing the scene in his mind and making a final picture of us all. With obvious pain he uttered the following words, "Children of France! Our country is at war. The Germans have just landed in Tunisia. The school is closed."

He stood there motionless; unable to say anything else, he gestured with his hand for us to go home. But no one budged. We left the lines very slowly. It was hard for us to understand the real meaning of the situation. Never before had our school seemed so dear to us, suddenly we loved it as we had never loved it before. My eyes wandered over and embraced the whole building as if to say goodbye to it, but like a last pilgrimage I walked back to my classroom, where I could read these few lines of our last song, left on the partly cleaned blackboard:

We are the children of Béja
A humble city of our great France
And we have already understood
That love . . .
Then, further on:
Let us walk with pride and joy,
Let us live in happiness
Let us live for France,
The land of immortality.

I read that last line, "the land of immortality" over and over, since to me it symbolized the grandeur of France. Then I went out to mingle with my schoolmates. We smiled at each other as if to gain confidence and courage. I was far from realizing that the glance my teacher, Mr. Vilmai, had given me that day was to be the last one. He was drafted and died a few months later.

Rumors said the British were coming, others said that they were Germans. We were poorly informed about either of them and their names were only known to us through history books.

At the thought of war, a feeling of mistrust came over us. We were unclear about what the future would hold for us. The Germans and the British were disturbing our childhood and our peaceful life.

Every day one could hear on the radio the Italian dictator Benito Mussolini, who was the head of the Italian government, saying, *"Io voglio la Tunisia,"* which meant, "I want Tunisia." It was a challenge to France, which had become weak after the German invasion. Among the population, the feelings were mixed. The French, the Jews and the Maltese were worried, while among the Italian residents some were hopeful. The feelings of the local Tunisians were also mixed, as some hoped that the French would lose and Tunisia would be free and others didn't trust any occupier. There were also those saying, "Better the occupiers we know than those we don't know."

FACTS

On Monday November 16, 1942, a German military delegation came to our town to give our Mayor, Jean Hugon, a 24-hour ultimatum to surrender the town. As a reaction to the ultimatum, the latter informed our civil governor, Mr. Clement, who in turn sent the message to Algiers. The next day, November 17, the first British battalion parachuted into the hills north of the town. Thursday November 19, German planes bombed our town for the first time, as a warning. This broke the long period of peace, Béja had known for many centuries. A day later, Friday November 20, Béja was furiously bombed by German airplanes for many hours, because of its key position leading to the roads of Tabarka, Mateur, Bizerte, and Algeria.

Contrôle civil, (regional government) Béja

THE DAY BOMBING STARTED

On Tuesday November 17, early in the morning, little men holding on to colorful balloons came down from the sky. The sky had become clouded with them. They were British parachutists.

"Brand new men from God, sent by our prophet," said Ali.

"No", answered Nicolas, "they are angels." Both were wrong. They were neither angels nor messengers from God.

"They are the vanguard of the Allies; better to see the British than the Germans," said our elders. We, the little ones, did not have any opinion. All of this was disturbing to us. We did not have the least desire to welcome anyone, and even less soldiers. The sky was downcast and menacing; the air was losing its purity. As if out of our books, a warlike spirit deriving from the earlier times of the Carthaginians, the Numidians and the Romans pervaded the atmosphere with a repulsive smell, which stifled the velvety perfume of lilacs and jasmine.

This feeling was suddenly interrupted by the news so feared by our grownups: the Germans had just reached Tunis; they were already holding all the cities along the coast. The grownups were sad and so was I. My vacations seemed to be in jeopardy. I was musing, remembering the beautiful summer days, the games on the warm sand, the waves stroking the young Arab, Italian, Jewish, French, and Maltese girls lying by the sea, some covered up, some in their bathing suits, the evenings on the beaches washed by the cool breezes of the Mediterranean, soothing our sunburnt bodies. I was recalling the merchants of *bonboloni* (doughnuts) coming out of nowhere at the time of day when the brightness of the sun diminishes as it sinks below the horizon. The ruins of

Carthage would appear in the background and that was the sign of the end of the day.

On Thursday November 19th, I went to the train station. I saw that British soldiers had occupied the engine shed which was empty at that time and were cleaning and maintaining their weapons and their belongings. In the afternoon, I was going home, when suddenly I heard a terrible noise. Planes were flying over the town; I counted seventeen; we had never seen so many at once. One of them, headed for the town, dropped a black object and flew up again. A terrifying sound burst out. When I arrived at home, my father, who was alarmed, explained to us what we had to do in the event that the planes came back the next day.

The next morning I went to see the British soldiers again. They were kind and they gave me candy. Suddenly more planes than the day before were in the sky. This time the noise was stronger than last time. This time for sure they were going to bomb our town and kill and destroy as much as they could.

*

Suddenly another explosion. I fainted. Mrs. Nino, a Maltese lady, brought me back to life by splashing a glass of water over my face. Waking up suddenly and seeing her next to me reminded me of an episode in Mr. and Mrs. Nino's life.

Josephine Nino was a simple and extremely kind person. She had practically never left the threshold of her home. Since she limped, she would spend most of her time seated on her wooden chair, by the window, watching the passersby. We, as children, became fond of her and she knew us all well. She had a tall, portly husband who was the driver of the horse-drawn carriage of the town. On the day of my communion, he drove us to the river in his carriage as was the custom.

He had two carriages: one for

weddings and the other for funerals. On those occasions he adorned his horses either with white or black ribbons. The horses were beautifully trained so that they could, according to the need of the occasion, assume a different pace, either proudly holding their heads high, with a joyful look or adopting a very slow and heavy gait with their heads lowered. Mr.

The Viaduct and the Pont Cinquième, three miles from Béja, where Mr. Nino the coachman would take us on festive occasions.

PHOTO BY EMILE SULTAN

Nino loved those two horses, since they were his source of income; he spent his days washing them, brushing them so that they were always ready to respond to any call.

Then, one winter, there was no wedding, no burial, which meant no income for Mr. Nino, who had to use his savings in order to live and to feed his horses. One day, Mr. Fratello, one of his friends, asked him to rent out his horses to work in the fields. At first, he felt insulted and answered, "Are you serious? My horses? They are trained like my children! Are you out of your mind?" Nino was adamantly opposed to the idea, but eventually, after much thought, he grudgingly accepted the suggestion since, being out of work, he was exhausting his savings. He accepted on two conditions: one to bring back his horses as soon as he would be called for a wedding or a funeral, and two not to overwork them.

Mr. Nino was sad at the thought of giving them up. After all, they were his best friends. He felt he was a coward and he was unable to face them.

On the first day, he walked them to their new job the same manner as one takes kids to school. He felt sad to see them off to work and from time to time he would interrupt their work so that they could rest. But this situation could not last much longer; Nino felt that his daily interventions could undermine his relationship with Mr. Fratello. Therefore he decided not to visit them anymore.

A few days later, one of the horses suddenly died. Mr. Fratello was devastated. How was he to break the sad news to Nino?

Mr. Manjoul was considered a wise man among the old Arabs in the city; he was respected, listened to and had the trust of the entire community. He never missed an opportunity to help others. Mr. Fratello went to consult him.

"What you are telling me here, Mr. Fratello," said Mr. Manjoul, "is very serious. I wonder whether Nino will be able to stand the shock. But don't consider offering him money, which he might resent even more. Let me have some time to think over this problem."

The following day, Mr. Manjoul asked the local magistrate to pay him a visit in order to inform him, and he asked him for a solution to this awful story. The magistrate was not comfortable dealing with this situation and thought it might have been a practical joke. Mr. Manjoul convinced him to the contrary and told him, "What you will have to do is very simple. Early tomorrow morning you will wake up Nino and you will ask him to come and see you at 8 a.m. When he arrives, you will tell him very tactfully that you dreamed that his eldest son, Antoine, was dead."

"And then?" asked the magistrate.

"The rest will be my responsibility" answered Mr. Manjoul.

The following day, they did as

it was arranged. To Mr. Nino's great astonishment, he received a very early call from the magistrate. For sure an important man must have died and the magistrate wanted to talk to him about the details of the funeral. The horses were not there but, never mind, he would deal with that later in the morning. At that moment he was visualizing the procession going through town with himself perched on his carriage, impeccably dressed in his top hat to the admiration of passersby. As she had been forewarned, Mrs. Nino got up and started cleaning and pressing her husband's beautiful black uniform which was hanging in the closet for such an occasion.

Nino arrived at eight o'clock sharp and was greeted by the magistrate with a serious expression on his face. Nino, guessing the cause of his seriousness, said, "Don't worry; I am always ready at any time to fulfill my duties."

"That's beside the point, my dear

Nino. I am overwhelmed and deeply distressed; I don't quite know how to tell you this, but I had a terrible nightmare, I dreamed of Antoine's death."

"Who? Antoine, my son?"

"Yes, my dear Nino, your son."

Overwhelmed and half crazed, Nino collapsed in an armchair. At that moment, someone knocked on the door. Mr. Manjoul, out of breath, appeared and said,

"Well, Nino, here you are, I've been looking for you everywhere." What on earth did Manjoul want? Probably to confirm Antoine's death. "My poor Nino, I have bad news for you," Manjoul added.

"Oh, my God! Don't tell me it is about my son Antoine."

"But who's talking about him. It's about one of your horses which has just died." As if ejected from the armchair, Nino jumped up with joy.

"One of my horses? What do I care! Thank God it's not my son." The magistrate, still playing his role, added,

"Well! There's still some truth to my dream, it was about your horse and not Antoine."

But Nino was already outside, on his way home singing and dancing. He had never been so happy in his whole life. Once more, Mr. Manjoul had succeeded in finding a happy solution to a serious problem.

Rue Kheireddine, a busy street in Béja.
On the left side, the house built by the Bellity family.

Mrs. Nino, who had taken me on her knee, patted me, put me on the ground and said, "Run back home, my son, it's wartime." I did not understand the full meaning of her words. I had never seen a war before.

*

Everybody was running away like sheep attacked by a wolf. Planes were flying low almost grazing the rooftops. There were explosions everywhere with terrifying noises mingled with screams and shrieks from injured people. I was afraid of being crushed by the panic-stricken crowd. Women and children were running in all directions. I no longer knew where I was. I was swept away in this human maelstrom and lost in eddies created by the *kashabeeas* and *melhafas* (very wide garments) of the Arabs. I was not sure in which direction to go. Then suddenly in this deafening uproar, there was total silence and I felt abandoned and alone. I saw myself as if in a well, and felt detached from this frantic human mass, from the streets and houses and from the church which I could no longer see. I sensed danger and became afraid. But the more fearful I became, the stronger I grew. I became a stranger to my body which had been caught up in the general panic.

Without realizing how far I had strayed, I found myself in front of our own house. I quickly went up the stairs; the door to our apartment was wide open. Not a soul was there, dishes were left on the table, which was covered with a wax cloth. A pot was on the charcoal fire, still burning strongly. My sister's slippers littered the hallway.

I was overcome by gloom. Dark thoughts entered my mind. I already saw myself as an orphan abandoned to a sad fate. Instinctively, I knocked on my neighbor's door which stood ajar. Only the cat was left and his expression showed abandonment. I returned to the empty street where I met only silence. I felt like crying and screaming, but to what purpose? I didn't know what to do, return home or go to school or to the synagogue, or to the church? I was at a loss. I knew I had to do something but I did not know exactly what. In this devastated town, I decided to go to my second home, the school. On my way over there, suddenly the environment had a very different quality: it was pleasant, scented, and human. Someone was following me. I turned around and immediately became very happy. My friend Fatma stood there smiling graciously. I jumped into her arms like a dog, seeing its master again, hugging her and not wanting to let go. She allowed me to do it; then after a while the sincere and noble look in her eyes seemed to indicate that she was bringing life back to me, that she was holding the most precious secret in the universe. Fatma knew where my mother was. "Go to your mother," she said in a soothing voice, "she is at your aunt's."

CHILDHOOD REGAINED

*

The vivid memory of that moment brings back recollections of Fatma's wedding. It followed traditions so different from today, when most of the rites have changed. The engagement was concluded by the parents and the couple to be did not meet until the wedding night. Age differences were frequent but parents were not concerned by this, only financial interest prevailed.

A few months before the war, Fatma and I were playing in the courtyard. She was wearing a green leaf printed dress which added something to her lovely figure. Her face was as round as a rosebud ready to burst open, her arms were plump, her braided long hair as black as a winter night. She exuded good health. She was carefree. While we were playing, her mother called to tell her that her engagement had just been concluded by her father and her father-in-law to be.

She came back very upset, on the verge of tears which clouded her beautiful eyes. However, she kept her composure to tell me that we had to stop playing. She had to give up childhood games and schooling and her life would change completely. She left me brusquely and ran to her room. I followed her. She was already crying. I tried to comfort her without knowing why I was doing it.

"It's over between us; we won't be able to play anymore. I have to become a woman and later on a mother." I did not understand why her marriage had to put an end to our relationship and to our games. And on top of that it was hard for me to see her as a mother. She was stroking her doll as if to say goodbye. Tomorrow it would be her husband she would have to stroke submissively. How could she oppose her father's decision? She had to obey him. She could not even give her opinion; everything was concluded between the two men, it was final and permanent. She had to love her husband unconditionally despite her youth and her need for tender care, now she would be the one providing care. She was brutally torn from her childhood without any intermediary stage. I shared her anguish, but I could not do anything to help or to defend her. Was it possible not to see Fatma again, Fatma, my playmate and my friend? Once married, she would lead a secluded life, isolated from everyone except much older women with whom she could not have anything in common.

"You," she said, "you are lucky, you are a boy, and then you are not a Muslim. You will be able to see, talk and go out with the woman who will become your wife." People envied her, but she was ready, if the opportunity arose, to give up that fiancé she had never seen or known. I heard the grownups say, "She will learn to love her husband," as if it could not be otherwise, as if love was to be learned, as if love and feelings were two different things.

Our street had been filled with joy and happiness during the seven days prior to her wedding. Carriages drawn by horses brought Fatma's trousseau ordered by her father. The social level of the bride in those days was evaluated according to the number of horses. Huge couscous dishes and whole sheep were brought in order to feed family members who had come from afar for the wedding. All the dressmakers in town had been hired and had been working for months on the dresses for the bride and for the guests. Weddings were a rare opportunity for the young ladies to parade in their long beautiful gowns decorated with embroidery. Women had their faces and legs waxed to remove hair with a mixture of warm water, sugar and lemon, the best cosmetic product known and used among Arab families. Women colored their hair with henna; they manicured their hands and feet. Young girls took advantage of the situation to have their ears pierced.

Before the wedding, there was the day of the Turkish bath. The morning was reserved for men and the afternoon for women. All the guests accompanied the new couple to this cleansing ceremony.

Children below the age of ten (and I was one of them) were accepted at the women's session. It was there that one whispered for the first time in the ears of the bride the practice of lovemaking. Experienced women quarreled over the honor of giving the best advice to Fatma who was red with shame. She was naked as everyone else; her body was plump, her skin as soft as a baby's. Women did not pay much attention to the young boys while we listened to what was said with an innocent attitude and did not miss an occasional glance at all those naked bodies. We thus became spies for men who did not miss an opportunity to question us on what we had seen or heard.

At the age of ten, we lost the privileges that the women had granted us. Then, we had to go to the men's baths where men covered their bodies with huge towels called "*fouta*". There the atmosphere was more serious, more austere at least for us. When men told stories, they made sure to send us away. They thought that only they were privy to life's secrets but of course we already knew them thanks to the women. Naturally we pretended not to understand anything, but we knew more than the men could suspect. They did not know for sure whether we were informed; in any case they preferred not to find out the truth about us. By sending us away the men were misjudging us, but also misleading us. And thus lying became a part of our life from puberty. We also had our own secrets learned at home, from neighbors, or elsewhere, which we exchanged. We were unseen witnesses and therefore knew everything that happened everywhere. We were like old trees which have stood witness to so many generations. If they could speak, they would teach us so many things about our ancestors. Like them, we remained silent, disclosing nothing, to avoid creating tragic situations within families.

Various customs preceded the religious ceremony, including that of a gold coin dipped in henna and put in the bride's left hand. These customs were omens for happiness in marriage. Everyone, close and distant friends of the two families, hoped to be invited to the final reception. For Fatma's wedding we were invited as well as all the neighbors. The reception took place at the bridegroom's parents' home. They owned a sumptuous villa. According to custom, men were in one room and women in another. My tender age allowed me to go everywhere. My mother took me with her to the room of the women, the walls of which were decorated with flowers and embroidered tapestries. The guests were seated on beautiful rugs which covered the whole floor; they leaned on silk or velvet cushions and talked. Mint tea was served in glasses from trays resting on top of low tables, together with cakes dipped in honey, and all kinds of non-alcoholic drinks and delicacies. Richly dressed in silk and tulle, Fatma moved from one group to the other, as a hostess, to the accompaniment of compliments and *youyou* sounds. She was very pretty with her big black eyes expressing joy and sadness at the same time. What was she to become? What would be her destiny? Would she be happy? She was hardly fifteen, still a child and her husband was over fifty. Using my privilege I went to the room reserved for men; they were talking with each other, some standing, others sitting; they were sipping tea and nibbling on cookies or other pastries. As he saw me, the bridegroom, who did not know his wife to be yet, urged me to describe her. "Is she pretty, tall, small, blond or dark haired?"

These questions bothered me but the

truth could disappoint him, so I answered, "She is very beautiful, noble, and as white as milk."

Later on, entertainment took place in the big illuminated garden where only men and older women were admitted. Young women and young girls watched the scene from a distance through the lattice windows of the villa. An orchestra played loudly accompanying the sensuous voices of the Oriental women singers. But the belly dancers were the focus of attention, wearing very little, virtually naked, they wriggled their bodies to charm the audience. Men's eyes were dazzled and overwhelmed by this abundance of female flesh.

This was Fatma, whom I had hugged on the day of the bombing. Her body had changed but her look had remained the same, sensitive and profound. However, it expressed resignation. The beginning of the war had not succeeded in changing her and she had become wiser and fulfilled her role as an Arab woman. She was faithful to her husband and their customs. She had kept the same smile I had always known. Her eyes had the placidity of well water. Her life progressed as if nothing of importance had happened. She had found peace and serenity in her isolation as an Arab wife. Her behavior had inspired me with security and confidence. Since that time I have not seen her, nor the other Arab girls I had met during my childhood.

Wealthy Arab residential interior

Fortunately, today traditions have changed. Young girls may discard the veil. They are the beneficiaries of an evolution Fatma would have appreciated in her own time.

*

My mother's innocence was such that it bordered on naiveté; she was fearful whereas my father was very brave. As he had foreseen continuous bombings, he had forbidden my mother to leave our home.

"Our house is strongly built," he said, "we are well protected, since it is made of stones and steel beams and cannot be easily destroyed." But this affirmation was not enough to reassure her. We lived on the second floor and she was frightened at the thought of being buried under the house.

As a result she chose to seek refuge at my aunt's place, which was not far from where we lived. She lived in an *oukala*, a house in the Arab style, built around a central courtyard. It had a large gate and individual rooms and was owned by my father's uncle. My aunt occupied one of the large rooms. We had spent beautiful days there with family or with my cousins. With the condition I was in, many memories came to me incoherently.

I ran to my aunt's. I knocked loudly on the door. The old owner of the house opened it slowly and greeted me with, "Well, here you are; your mother is in the room over there with all the cowards. They are afraid of dying, but not I." The room was crowded. The children were weeping; women did not stop invoking all the prophets and the saints.

The only man who was there was my uncle. He was also panic stricken. He kept repeating, "My God! I don't want to die this way," which brought to my mind the following question, "Was there another way in which he would like to die?"

CHILDHOOD REGAINED

My father came home very late that day; it was his habit to go shopping for Shabbat. As soon as he had finished, he was paralyzed with fear from the gunfire of the planes flying low overhead and shooting pitilessly at everyone on the streets. He took shelter in the store of a building which seemed strong. When calm returned, he went home. There he found no one despite the instructions given to my mother. Guessing where we all were he went to my aunt's with his big shopping basket full of provisions: meat, tripe, fruits, vegetables, cakes dipped in honey, almonds, pistachios, etc. Unfortunately it was already night and as we had entered the Shabbat, the women were not allowed to cook. Instead of dinner, we had to nibble on anything not requiring preparation, after saying the usual Friday prayers, which while not hurried through, lacked the solemnity with which our elders usually endowed them.

On the following day at about 9 o'clock, a new wave of German planes skimmed over the houses while mercilessly bombing and raking the streets with machine gunfire. The dead and wounded lay on all sides. Our anti-aircraft defense was not responding. But did it actually exist? As soon as we heard the roaring of the planes above our heads, we were filled with fear, which aggravated our permanent anguish. We would embrace and ardently kiss each other as if to say goodbye. Fortunately the menace of death would leave us as quickly as it came. The survivors from the streets who ran for shelter to my aunt's brought with them awful news of the latest casualties. A friend had lost his father that same day and entire families were buried under debris. People in need of shelter swamped my aunt's and her neighbors' rooms. The courtyard was filled with people, since the *oukala* had been spared together with a few buildings.

Then came the night with its protecting veil of darkness, which seemed to us all too fleeting under those circumstances. The elderly got together and decided that we should go and spend the night at the synagogue where many families had taken refuge. Everyone agreed, thinking it was better to die closer to God. On the contrary, I thought it was better to live closer to God.

The exterior wall of the synagogue and interior tiles

The new church of Béja, built in 1938

ASSESSING THE DAMAGE IN OUR STREET

The neighboring houses were destroyed. All one could see were piles of stones. Streets were strewn with all kinds of debris, housewares and pieces of furniture, all completely destroyed. Terrified crowds were running in all directions looking for shelter. Now that so many houses had been destroyed, one could have a complete perspective of our small town with its church still standing in the center. After each "all clear", shelters would empty and the people would emerge completely drained mentally and physically.

In our town, war had ended after the Vandals. The Byzantines had rebuilt it, and with the passing of time it had become a beautiful and important center in the region. Was it going to be besieged once more? There was not much left to be saved. My imagination wandered and went back to the seventh century when the Arabs had conquered it and converted its people to Islam with the power of the sword. Were we on the verge of being overtaken by the Germans and maybe having to learn their language instead of our French language?

To the extensive Roman ruins, of which we were so proud, were added the newly created ruins of so many houses. Dust from destroyed buildings was hanging heavily in the air. A smell of burnt blood rose up in the clear sky as if to show the world the horror of what we were going through.

Death did not scare us anymore but physical pain was haunting us. The suffering of the wounded people was extremely hard to endure. None of us knew what death meant. We were watching other people's death, never our own. We were weeping for the loss of others but actually we were weeping for ourselves, in anticipation. It is difficult to understand enigmas, and death is one of them. Church bells no longer tolled for the dead but chimed for those still alive.

We had the whole night in front of us. Never had I realized that the night was such a friend and the darkness no longer frightened me. Dead bodies were indistinguishable in the ruins. We had been told so many tales about the dead, which scared us. And there they were, lying still, no longer scaring me. Fear, I believe, is induced by the behavior of the living. They obey orders blindly and often act against their own heart and mind while serving causes they do not espouse. They kill and are not even aware of the atrocity of their acts. They are ordered by cruel superiors whose ambition stifles human feeling.

Around the town square, ruined houses had been converted into cemeteries. I could not see the point of killing so many defenseless people and destroying so many houses. Those planes with their bombs were destroying our paradise, our soccer game, and scattering our team and our friends all over the world.

All of us, Muslims, Christians, Jews had lived on excellent terms. We were like brothers. Fridays, Saturdays and Sundays were holy days. We as children would use the streets as soccer fields. I belonged to a team. We would mark goal posts with stones. Soccer balls were difficult to find so we made them out of fabric. My friend Victor's father who was a shoemaker sewed the outside with shoe leather. Marino, our Italian friend brought back pig guts from the slaughterhouse for the inner bladder; all we had to do was inflate it. From time to time we would all together go around to the mosques, the synagogues and the churches in order to keep our team going. Usually friends would wait outside for those who were inside the sanctuary. But one Saturday they decided to come with me to the synagogue, because on that day we had a very important soccer game; there was no way we could have split. The rabbi was overjoyed at seeing so many young people; he came to me and asked, "My son, who are all these young people?"

I responded, "They are my cousins from the city of Sousse who are spending their vacation with me."

One Sunday, we all went to church since we did not want to leave François, our best right wing player. The priest who was as short-sighted as the rabbi asked the same question to which François gave a similar response.

Certainly we tricked the rabbi and the priest but without any ulterior motive. Those preachers of the Truth would never have understood our truth; still we felt dishonest and ashamed. Remorse weighed on us since we had all lied. But was there another way to ensure we would have a full team for our game? The rabbi and the priest both preached fine sermons, only with different individual presentation, style and substance. In fact, one as well as the other believed in their truth. They both had different viewpoints while ours suited us, as we did not discriminate between our religions.

One day, Raymond who was very respectful towards religion and the clergy, called us together and suggested that we tell the rabbi and the priest the truth of our situation. We all objected because we felt that these old gentlemen were living with their beliefs and telling them the truth would disturb them.

Everyone finds happiness in what they believe to be true. The important thing is to be honest with oneself. Despite our subterfuge we did not object to the company of the priest and the rabbi. We liked to question them, although we were indifferent to their advice; we knew in advance that it would not satisfy us. We were amused by their different responses to identical questions. But we were fond of them; they were part of our childhood, just as other people were in our little town. They shared our life and era. An era is a period of time where, as in a play, people are acting out roles against the backdrop of a stage set. As the play changes, so do the actors and the stage setting. For us, the little town was the stage, its people were the actors and "Era" was our play. Memory alone can recall the stage set but it is impossible to recreate the atmosphere of the play without involving the personal emotions of the bygone era. That's why each of the actors keeps a different image of the era they experienced together.

EMILE TUBIANA

Fields around Béja

CHILDHOOD REGAINED

OUR DESPERATE SEARCH FOR A SAFE PLACE

The bombing lasted until nightfall. My aunt's house was adjacent to the synagogue where we spent another night. Our elders' prayers were mixed with women's laments and children's cries. Almost all of the Jewish survivors joined us there.

At dawn, many families started to disperse. My father, as a French veteran, became the moral leader of those remaining, but he had no idea where to go. Under such circumstances, the countryside seemed to offer more security than the city. In my father's judgment it was vital to leave before the return of the bombers and therefore we left the city heading off for the country. We had hardly reached the top of the hill outside the city when two planes appeared heading in our direction. My father shouted, "This time, they will get us." They were flying so low that we could see the pilots clearly. They went up again flying over the town and came back towards us. It looked as though they took pleasure in scaring us. We were at the mercy of armed people and since we had no choice, we were prepared to die each time a plane came near us, but fortunately they flew away.

We continued our journey and came across a path into the country. Although we were of different ages, we all walked quickly as if leaving the town protected us from death. We walked silently, breathing in the pure air of the country and the smell of the fields. Our little town was disappearing below the horizon. We had never walked so far and we were not familiar with the beautiful countryside around our town, which these attacks forced us to discover. A large horse-drawn cart appeared on the path and my father waved to stop it. After negotiating with the driver, women and children were allowed to get on board. The wheels with big wooden spokes scared me because a child's head or foot could easily get caught. The possibility of such an accident frightened me more than the bombing we had gone through. In the evening we arrived in Zaouiet Medien, now called "Zahret Medien" (The Rose of Medien), a village, entirely inhabited by Arabs, where most houses were built of clay mixed with straw, and a few were of stone. The sheikh, the head of the village, received us with a cold welcome. He took us to a huge warehouse, which was already occupied by refugees who had arrived a few hours before us. Only women and children were allowed inside; men had to sleep outside in the open air.

The women in our group demarcated the area which was allocated to us and laid down blankets on the floor. Children started to cry for food but unfortunately we had no food and the sheikh could only offer us a shelter. However, an old

Jewish woman, her name was Rhayma, approached the children with a little bag in her hands and took them outside; they followed her like a swarm of bees following their queen. Her little bag was precious since it held macaroni. The children were happy as they were going to eat.

"We are going to cook good pasta in water", she said. "Bring me some wood." Needless to say she had a big pile in a very short time and with stones she built some kind of hearth. She realized then that there was no cooking pot and asked the children to find one but in vain. However, a girl had a chamber pot which was cleaned and used as a replacement. We were all gathered around the fire and waited impatiently for the food to be ready. The old woman stirred the macaroni from time to time with a stick. Waiting made us even hungrier and whetted our appetite. She kept us quiet assuring us there would be a wonderful meal. In fact there was only macaroni without salt, tomatoes or butter.

Some of the men got busy clearing the empty cans that British soldiers had left behind. We used them as dishes, finding it amusing. We were no longer thinking of our home, our comfort, regular dishes; farewell to the one, farewell to the other, farewell to everything…

Later, while standing at the back of the warehouse, I felt lonely. The door was open and the intense darkness of the night, unfamiliar to city people, was oppressive to me. For the first time, I could hear my heartbeat. From time to time, I caught sight of the glow of a cigarette and this reassured me.

Even though I tried hard, I could not fall asleep, despite the emotions and the fatigue of the day. The noises of the bombs, the planes, the sirens and the moaning of the wounded remained in my ears. On top of this, the shrill crying of a baby whom the women could not calm and lull to sleep was deeply disturbing, it went right to my heart, and quite overwhelmed me. I would have preferred to relive the horrors of the last few days rather than be subjected to the screams of an innocent baby who could not find his peace in the tormented world in which he was born.

Could we expect some humanity from our enemies? Humaneness is an empty expression which we use when it is convenient. Mankind continues to kill blindly, even more brutally, almost to the point of total destruction. Humanity doesn't exist anymore. It took with it what's most beautiful and precious in this world, peace and love. These are mankind's most fundamental needs. Peace allows people to come together, regardless of race, color and religion. We are all human. However love and peace are not served to us on a silver platter. It is not enough to want them, we have to struggle in order to create them and, as a start, we have to eradicate from our minds the mistrust which engenders evil. Never mind my neighbor who may disapprove and not do anything in this vein. His attitude does not relieve me from my responsibilities. He may criticize me and say that I am a dreamer. I would certainly be hurt; naturally we always prefer praise. I may even weep, but a word which makes us shed tears often provides food for thought for correction and for improvement, and therefore has positive consequences. A word which provokes laughter does not lead to constructive thought.

After a few days spent in this Arab village, my father could not bear seeing his children with so little food and comfort and decided to go back to town.

"If it is written that we should die from the bombing it may happen anywhere, so we might as well be home," he said.

The idea of returning was frightening to us. Was it possible to go back willingly to the fear, anxiety and horrors we had gone through? But my father was right, we had no choice, my younger brother was sick with bronchitis and in that village there was neither doctor nor medicine. And to further convince us, he added, glancing at my mother holding my brother in her arms, "If he dies, we would not be able to bury him according to our rites, the cemetery is reserved to Muslims."

This time we found a cart with good tires. Families who had come with us refused to leave this safe but unwelcoming village. The return journey took less time. On the way we met many British soldiers. Anti-aircraft defenses hidden with nets and branches were set-up in the fields.

"I guess they are in charge to protect our town from German airplanes," said my father happily, using any positive event to reinforce his arguments. From afar we saw planes bomb our city. Instinctively the driver slowed down his horse. Our fear grew by the minute, as we advanced. My mother curled up in one corner in order to protect my brother who rested on her lap sheltered from the cold wind. She looked at my father imploringly and he sensed her distress without her saying a word. My father reacted immediately.

"Fine," he said, "we'll stay outside the city until nightfall." We were relieved by his decision. Naively we thought pilots slept at night and therefore would not drop bombs. Danger was temporarily set aside. At nightfall we entered the city on foot. Streets were deserted and dark. Guided by our father we avoided military patrols by walking through narrow side streets; there was a curfew.

"Hurry up!" said my father as our steps resounded loudly on the paving stones and broke the oppressive silence. The noise was echoing, as the streets were empty and my father was very impatient, leading all his kids in the dark. We could hardly see each other and he was eager to see us safe in a shelter. We finally reached my aunt's house that we had left after the first day of bombing. We were looking forward to seeing known faces and family members. It did not take long to be disappointed, the house was empty, and everyone had left for the country. The warmth created by all those people had vanished and died out as had the lives of many dear friends.

The old man, my father's uncle, had remained, determined to die at home rather than to "kick the bucket" outside like a dog. He asked us to join him in his spacious room. But we stood motionless on the threshold when we saw on the ground a human shape under a white cloth.

"Well, it's better this way," explained the old man. "The poor woman! At least for her it was a natural death. I had met her running in all directions in the streets, completely panicked. She had lost her family and I offered her hospitality. To thank me, she wanted to be useful so she took care of the household, of the kitchen. Yesterday after teatime, she did not feel well and I advised her to rest but she assured me that it was neither the time to be sick nor to die. She did not like the idea of my being alone. What was the good of telling her I could also die? Overwhelmed with fatigue, she fell asleep and she never woke up. That's a beautiful way of dying! How fortunate to die in your sleep! Tomorrow you'll help me bury her." We had listened to him religiously but deep down I did not share his viewpoint, I felt it was better to die and be aware of it.

Two old women who knew someone had died came for the wake. Therefore we all spent the night seated on the floor around the body. The old man's feet bumped occasionally into the head of the poor woman. Sleep overtook each of us in turn but for a short while only. My mother however did not sleep at all; she was affected by the scene of the wake. She was worried about my young brother and continued to hold him tightly in her arms.

During the night the noises of plane

engines and those of fresh bombing and of the anti-aircraft defense, overwhelmed the city, then suddenly everything was silent again. I had the feeling of being in another world. I had never known such complete silence and such a dark night. I started thinking of life, of the good and the bad it has to offer, simply of its meaning. My sisters were sound asleep but I wanted to stay awake to take advantage of life. Why should I sleep? Such moments are precious and one must live them. I could not imagine that a bomb could interrupt the course of our lives. I felt something very enduring in me that nothing could destroy.

THE CLUB OF THE FEARFUL

After the hurried burial of the poor woman, we realized that we were the only survivors in the center of our town formerly so crowded but now deserted and virtually destroyed. My mother became more and more worried by this isolation. She said that if she were to be dying she would wish to be surrounded by many people and by the familiar noises of an active community. I disagreed—when one dies, one dies alone. In the mind of the dying person, the coming of death suppresses any cognizance of his surroundings, for he leaves this world in silence and solitude; at least that was the way I thought about it.

My father decided to take us to the other side of town which was less exposed to danger. However it appeared that danger was everywhere, with daily air raid alerts and bombings. We took shelter in another courtyard house in the Italian neighborhood, where the houses were built on a slope and gave us the impression of being protected. My father thought that the Germans were less likely to bomb Italians since they were allied with Italy. This house was located in the vicinity of my Uncle Victor's house. We joined other families but the feeling of discomfort and anxiety remained. My father grieved to see us in such conditions. Because the only kitchen was too small for all the families, the mothers had to take turns to work there. The only advantage of being there was the presence of a dedicated nurse who took care of my sick brother, who eventually recovered.

Alfred, my father's cousin, was among us refugees at the courtyard house. He was a painter by trade, well respected, a large and strongly built man. For fun, he would lift up bags of hundred kilos (two hundred twenty pounds). Unfortunately his morale was broken by the war and he became pessimistic and increasingly fearful. One day he reacted very angrily to a sarcastic remark by my father and said, "What can we do against a bomb? Nothing, but if you give me a bull or the strongest man, I'll put them down in the blink of an eye." He was constantly panic stricken, infecting others who lived in fear. He set up a group that panicked at each alert. He was nicknamed the "King of the Fearful" and nobody contested his title. One day he called a meeting to which the few residents remaining in the neighborhood were invited and he said, "Dear brothers and sisters, you've seen with your own eyes what has happened and what's still going on. It is therefore useless to further describe the horrors that we are witnessing. We need to find a way to protect ourselves. A trench is a good shelter for our protection from bombing attacks and I believe we should dig one.

Go back to your homes and bring back any useful tools and if the planes leave us alone for a few hours, with God's help, we'll finish it. In this way if we die it won't be under debris." My father asked him mockingly whether we should paint the trench, to which Alfred replied calmly, "Let's keep it for the tombs."

Young and old, we all started to work with enthusiasm. Alfred had convinced us that a trench was our salvation. It took a whole day to dig it. It had a bend. After completion, I realized we had not chosen an ideal spot since it was located near a camp of British soldiers which seemed a good target for the enemy bombers. I wondered whether Alfred chose it on purpose, in order to be close to the army and thereby protected. I was too young to criticize him but nevertheless I realized that fear leads to illogical actions. Fear has never elevated man but brings him down in the eyes of others. If Alfred were to die in the trench, he would not die alone. We would die with him and that to him would be comforting. This did not offer comfort to me. Fear can lead to many unnecessary deaths. In contrast, courage can save people. A general, brave and confident, may lead an army to victory with limited losses, but on balance many people will be saved from death. Death captures those who run away but those who face it win. The haunting image of death has always been instilled in us together with the panic preceding it and the grief that follows. It would have been better to prepare ourselves for death rather than lose reality in illusory games and pleasures. What is the point of numbing the human spirit, which sooner or later will be confronted with the realities of existence?

After the completion of the trench, Alfred stayed there day and night. Pretending to be dead he would not seek to live. Because she was deaf, his wife Marie hardly realized what was going on; she could not hear the siren, nor the bombing.

During air raid alerts she saw us running to the trench and she was surprised. She stood on the doorstep wondering what kind of game we were playing. It was only when she saw the planes that she realized what was going on. After a while she spontaneously would look up at the sky as soon as she saw us rushing to the trench.

Alfred became the self-appointed leader followed by all the young people. I was the only one left from our courageous little group. Out of loneliness I too joined Alfred. I was sworn in according to the rules and became a full member. From that time on I had to obey Alfred's orders, since he was the only one who directed operations during these alerts. We had to shelter from bombers hiding at the bottom of the trench. We would repeat his prayers after him, "Abraham our father, Isaac his son, Jacob, Israel, the Holy Spirit, protect us all, God of all men, protect us, God of the Jews, God of the Christians and God of the Muslims, protect us." Personally,

I found those prayers ridiculous and one day I burst out laughing. For this insult I was severely beaten, in order to appease the Gods.

In order to eat we had to leave the trench, taking turns. Alfred would never budge since Marie brought him food. Each of us had guard duty in a spot protected from noise to detect the first signs of incoming bombers and to be able to warn those who for one reason or another were outside the shelter by day or by night. They were supposed to immediately go to the trench. Those who did not heed the warning were expelled from the group. I was overzealous as a member of the group, always first in the trench. In my spells of duty I enjoyed mixing real with false alerts. Alfred appreciated my obedience and my loyalty.

My father followed me in joining our group. He did it not out of fear but because of inactivity. Alfred was delighted with his membership since my father was regarded as the spiritual leader of the neighborhood and therefore enhanced Alfred's prestige. My father complied with Alfred's rules and did not feel at all diminished by the situation.

One cold and wet night my father assumed his first turn of duty. Everyone went to sleep reassured that my father was watching. Even Alfred was at ease. In the middle of the night my father heard planes approaching. He decided that it was best not to wake us up but to let us sleep and relax. Unfortunately a few minutes later a terrifying explosion shook us out of our sleep. Alfred was furious with my father. He kept a grudge against him and did not talk with him for a few days.

One evening, poor Marie brought her husband his usual meal during an air raid. Tense because of the danger, he threw the soup at her face. This enraged me. I shouted that he was a coward and his strength came only from dealing with weak people. He tried to hit me but I ran away from the trench. He followed me outside and finally caught up with me. Believe it or not, all this took place during an air raid! What a surprise to see him out of the trench, unprotected. I expected to be beaten up but to my great surprise he hugged me and said, "My child, your insult taught me a lesson and my deep-seated fears have gone now. I know now that I can lead the life of a normal man fully aware of his resources and capabilities. No need to panic in front of danger. You'll see everything will be fine." I became aware that a man can possess within himself latent power revealed only under particular circumstances.

As in any other town, City Hall was the center for food distribution. Every week, we would use our ration cards on specific days. This became an opportunity to meet other families and exchange the latest news about parents, friends, and acquaintances. Our bread rations came from Algeria, and even though the bread was hard and moldy, no one complained because we were grateful to receive it at all. Marie's deafness brought about situations that kept us laughing for a long time. One day, it was her and my mother's turns to pick-up the rations at City Hall for the families who lived at the courtyard house. Halfway there, they were taken by surprise by an air raid alert. When my mother shouted into Marie's ear to run for shelter, she answered, "I heard that they will distribute potatoes today." Seeing that it was hopeless, my mother started running as fast as she could. Marie agreed, "You are right, let's hurry-up to be among the first there, I will join you!"

Weeks went by. Our living conditions were awful: daily air raids, bombings that made us anxious and tense, and a situation exacerbated by the British soldiers who went after our women at nighttime.

CHILDHOOD REGAINED

NECESSITY

During WWII my father used to bring us bread
To the farm, far from the bombs over our head.
Our town was under constant aerial attack
We had fled it by night, each carrying a sack.

Everywhere the dead and wounded were lying
We had seen many friends and neighbors dying.
One day we were scared,
   we saw father from afar
Walking with a bag full of bread and a jar.

I asked, "Father, how did you walk
   the miles so fast?"
Tired, exhausted, from aerial and artillery blast
He answered, "My son, hunger and fear
Teach us to walk and to run for those dear."

Since, I understood that necessity is our guide
As it teaches us which way to decide.
The best decisions I made until now
Were those where necessity showed me how.

Farm on the outskirts of Béja

ON THE NEZER FARM

One evening, my cousin Lilo, my father's oldest sister's son, came to the house where we were staying. I didn't know how he had been able to find us under such circumstances. He came from a farm whose owner had been his customer for a paint job. When the bombing had started, he took his mother and his father to the farm. The farmer was very kind and hospitable. He opened the door to the refugees. As every family was scattered in different directions by the bombings, we never knew where everyone was. Feeling safe on that farm, his mother had sent him to look for her brother and to bring him to the farm, as she was very worried for him and his large family. My cousin convinced my father to go with him and to take refuge on the farm. My father could not take the situation in town any longer. He decided to let Lilo lead us to the distant farm where we could find refuge among other family members and friends who had been there since the beginning of the bombings.

It was difficult to cross the whole town in order to get to the path leading to the farm. Every night there was a curfew. We were told British patrols circulated everywhere to avoid loitering and to protect the few civilians who remained in town.

Because of the frequent bombings it was wise to start our journey at night. On our way through the empty streets we heard British patrols which we had to avoid since we were under curfew. At times, from our instant hiding places, we could see them stop at a bombed site, sorting through the debris in the hope of finding some precious object. Then we would resume our journey, each of us with a heavy bundle of blankets and cooking utensils which made up our basic needs. The trip was a few miles long and tedious. Our bags were heavy, we were tired and sleepy. From time to time we would discard some articles to lighten the load. My youngest sister who was three years old had difficulty keeping up with us. At times we lost sight of her; we had to stop frequently. Waiting for her gave us a brief rest, but she was exhausted; someone had to carry her. My mother was already carrying the baby and therefore my father put my sister on his shoulders and discarded his bundle. Miraculously we came across a herd of donkeys led by an old man at a point when we were all completely exhausted. The negotiation was short. In exchange for a few coins that my father handed him, the old man put his animals at our disposal. We transferred our loads and were relieved to walk side by side with the animals. Our pace picked up. While carrying the loads, we had not paid attention to the landscape, but then, relaxed, we were able to look at our surroundings and appreciate the pure air that invigorated us and the beautiful fields, as far as the eye could see, covered with a green carpet of thick grass and to enjoy the lazy sunrise and complete silence. No humming planes, no gloomy sirens.

Around noon we reached the Nezer farm which had become communal housing for thirty families. We were warmly welcomed with hugs and kisses. The French farmer had set aside a stable as a dormitory and delivered a cartload of hay as bedding for us. The stable was far away from the actual farm. The latter served a double purpose as it hid American and British reconnaissance pipers used to fly towards the German lines and back immediately. There were British intelligence officers living at that farm.

Everyone tried to make us feel at home, they warmed us up with a rich soup after our tiring journey. At last we felt secure. As children we were so happy to be there; life in the country was as though we were playing hooky from school. It was wonderful.

One day a cousin of mine came from town. He told us that his sister was staying in a brothel. Hearing this, his mother slapped him for saying such a word, not knowing that due to lack of space in hospitals, schools and brothels had been converted into makeshift infirmaries, due to a typhus epidemic.

Typhus! Another problem! Due to poor hygiene, the epidemic was spreading rapidly and death rates were rising. Again fear and anxiety were disturbing our tranquility. A British army physician by the name of Dr. Smith visited the countryside in order to trace the disease and attempt to control its spread. He isolated a few cases and sent them back to the city. Fortunately he was helped by a young Jewish physician from our town, by the name of Dr. Cohen. Thanks to his selfless dedication he saved the lives of many patients. We waited eagerly for his visits since he would bring us news about our friends remaining in the city. Unfortunately this was too often unpleasant and disturbing, such as hearing about the hospitalization of the whole Lelouf family in our former school. It was not difficult for us to understand the reason.

That news brought back to my mind the day when our principal told us we were at war. I remember my teacher, Mr. Vilmai, who had arrived from France full of enthusiasm for his teaching. He did not exercise strict discipline and showed us considerable friendliness. That did not endear him to his colleagues. He was adverse to making us write "I will not arrive late to school" a hundred times as punishment, believing that each mistake had its reason. His practice was to ignore infractions, but after class to ask us for an explanation on a one-to-one basis. In a very short time, our class became the best behaved and this was achieved without effort or punishment, much to the envy or even jealousy of the other teachers. Before class he would talk with us casually about anything, for example if we had a problem in fielding our soccer team he would volunteer and play with us; or if one of us had not fully understood a lesson he would give us extra time at his home. We were all familiar with his house since we all had had the pleasure of visiting him there. He would engage in free conversations as a way of opening our minds to new horizons and a greater understanding of life. It comes as no surprise that in such a nurturing environment we would become excellent students.

Mr. Vilmai was conscripted as a pilot as soon as war was declared. He was killed during his first mission, which saddened us greatly.

Typhus did not spare my uncle. We refused to see him go to die in a school or a brothel. Therefore, we all agreed to hide him during Dr. Cohen's usual visit. Later we heard that Dr. Cohen died of typhus as a result of his devotion. We knew it was risky and that we could be contaminated but we had accepted the idea of dying. The disease was merciless and destroyed entire families. It was similar to a hurricane leaving behind piles of corpses which we then had to carry to the cemetery. Even many of those who thought themselves spared already carried the virus. We did not count on the rare miracles of medicine. Our elders were convinced that no one could escape it. The British soldiers as well as our people were hit by the disease. Those who came looking for girls at the farm ran off in a second at the sound of the word "typhus". They would have been better off by staying in their own country. It was an ironic situation. Even if the German High Command had a good campaign plan, they were nevertheless greatly assisted by this epidemic.

THE FRONT LINE IS COMING CLOSER

We heard some news about the atrocities committed by the Germans against the Jews—which we had not previously known. The Tunisians looked at the Germans as their liberators and in sympathy endowed them with the expression "Hadji" which is a title of honor given to any Muslim upon his return from his pilgrimage to Mecca. As for us, we had termed the American and the British soldiers "Khamous" which is a Jewish first name we would use, since it was unsafe to call them by their real name in a pro-German environment.

The Germans increased their air raids, but we stayed outside of the farm buildings, as we were more afraid of typhus than of bombing. One day I recall watching aerial dogfights. We were stupidly following their attacks, as if it were a soccer game. The pilots tried to place their planes behind each other in order to have a better target. Whenever one of them succeeded they were alternately applauded by the French and the Jews or by the Arabs according to their loyalties. This scene saddened me since I knew that these two men in the sky were fighting for survival, and one of them would probably die leaving his family bereft. It was foolish to think that they would stop fighting.

Suddenly the British pilot positioned himself behind the German and fired at him. The German plane wrapped in a black cloud headed down to the ground. It was heartbreaking to watch. I was relieved to see the German opening his parachute. There was hope he would see his family again, although he might be held prisoner for a while! Unfortunately the English pilot, not satisfied, fired at the parachute. The German's head fell on his chest and his body thumped to the ground with a leaden sound.

British soldiers, French people from the farm and Jewish refugees ran out to rescue the body of that poor fellow who died for his *Vaterland und Freiheit* (homeland and freedom). In fact he died because his superiors sent him into battle. A small bible was found in his pocket but that did not help him very much. For sure, the British pilot had one too. I was wondering which God they were worshipping—probably the same.

In the afternoon a brief ceremony was held and three salvos were fired in salute by a British platoon to honor the dead pilot. What a farce! Jesus had just been buried again.

His parents would be notified by an elegant piece of paper saying "Your son is missing" or "Your son died for his country." They would never see him again. But I saw him alive and dead. He was too young to die; he knew death before knowing life.

Train map of northern Tunisia

CHILDHOOD REGAINED

FLEEING TO NOWHERE

I had been happy on this farm as I ran through wheat fields breathing in the fresh country air. Without going to school and not having any homework, I felt I was on an endless vacation. Life could not have been sweeter.

But from far away, we could hear the sound of the explosions of the homes and we could see the smoke coming out of the burning houses in our town. We were surrounded by bombing day and night. Although at that age I was not afraid of the arrival of the Germans at our borders, the heads of families felt differently and decided to resume their journey "to escape the danger" as they said. My father did not share their view. As a former French soldier he felt that there was no point in continuing to walk on without knowing our final destination. My mother begged him to go with the others. Her thought was that if we were to die, we should die together with those we know. My father finally accepted her argument although he was not convinced.

Once again, bundles on our shoulders, we took to the road. From time to time I looked back at my cherished farm, so filled with happy memories. Farewell! Farewell! Finally I could not see it any more. I walked with the others, but against my will. We did not know whether we would find a safe shelter on the way. Was this move the last one? No one had any idea. So there we were, propelled along by fate, like seeds blown away by the wind, in unknown directions. What power did we have to oppose this stream which swept us along?

I did not quite understand what we were running away from; since the Germans were still almost completely surrounding us. Pain, perhaps—or death?

What guarantee did we have? Suffering and death were everywhere. We believed we had well thought it over and made the right decision, but in reality, we didn't know anything.

After many hours of walking and late into the night, we arrived at Mastouta train station, about seven miles south of Béja. The scene was devastating; the main building had been destroyed as well as many train cars, which gave us an idea of the extent of the bombings.

The presence of a huge number of American soldiers going to the battlefront of Bizerte completed the warlike atmosphere. Is this the safe shelter? My father whispered, "Well, we wanted to defeat death when we were at the farm, and now we may well find it among these ruins and in this cold weather."

The American soldiers seemed to be busy. This was the first time I caught a glimpse of them. They looked taller to me than the British. Their appearance reminded me of the last class we had with Mr. Vilmai, our teacher, when we were told that France had helped the Americans free themselves from their most feared enemies of that time, the British. So now, in turn, the Americans alongside the British were helping France. This seemed odd to me. The soldiers were getting ready to go to Bizerte, the most crucial point of the battle. It seemed absurd to me that these soldiers had come from so far, at the risk of losing their lives, whereas we were desperately trying to find a peaceful spot.

The station was bustling with people: American, British, French soldiers coming from Algeria, and some returning from the battlefront of Bizerte. The moaning of wounded soldiers coming from every direction, members of fragmented families running between the train tracks looking for their loved ones, French civil servants and nurses hurrying in many directions. I held my sister's hand tightly in order not to lose her, since the other family members were out of sight. I could not see them because there was a blackout in the entire area. Once in a while some soldiers walked by with a lantern. This was the only way to realize that a human being was walking. This scenery saddened me very much.

The stationmaster, who used a wooden shack as his office, managed to gather all the families who had come from the farm. He offered us shelter in the only available freight car. First women and children were allowed in, and then the men, some of whom had great difficulty standing for lack of space. A few of them were sitting in the opening with their feet dangling outside. There was no way one could close the sliding doors.

The thought of a small German bomb thrown at us made me shiver! The way we were squeezed together, we would not even have time to get out. Wouldn't we have been better off staying on the farm? I asked myself. My mother was holding my baby brother in her arms. He was born just a few months before the bombing and was very tiny. He didn't know what calm meant, nor did he have a crib. My mother was sitting on the floor of the railroad car with her back to the wooden side panel. We could not move a foot or an arm and there was little air for breathing. A woman fainted, and suddenly a wet handkerchief landed on her face, thrown from a mysterious hand. My youngest sister Andrée was uncomfortable and cried for food. She hardly understood what was going on.

We were told that we were to be sent to a safe area. The question was whether we would be able to last until then, since we were exhausted from our walk, glued together like sardines in a can, and badly shaken up by the sight of war at the station. Occasionally our car was moved back and forth by the train engine, which gave us false hopes. Actually it was not until dawn that we finally got under way.

With increasing speed, the fresh country air forced its way into our car, and that felt good. We did not quite know where we were going. Was it really towards Algeria or merely towards another Tunisian city? All we cared about at that point was that we were moving and the air was refreshing our faces. I liked the pleasant sight of the meadows and of the mountains, of a green I had never seen before, interrupted by the tunnels we passed through. From the opposite direction we passed trains loaded with soldiers. Again, these men were going to their death, while we were heading towards the unknown.

Sometimes the train stopped in the middle of a tunnel. The train driver must have received an alert or he may have seen a plane. These stops would sometimes last a half an hour to an hour. This was the safest way to avoid being bombed by a German plane. It was dark in the tunnel and the children started crying.

EMILE TUBIANA

Souk-Ahras and Ghardimaou train stations

CHILDHOOD REGAINED

ON THE TRAIN

In the afternoon, the train reached a station after difficult traveling conditions. No one knew where we were. The train stayed there for a long time, allowing us to get out of the car and stretch a little, or to lie down outside wherever we could and take a nap.

My father explored the area and spoke with a worker. He found out that we were in the city of Souk-Ahras in Algeria. We were not allowed to go very far. At nightfall we were still in the same spot. Nevertheless, once the bright lights coming from the city indicated that we were past the frightening zones, we were no longer fearful. There were no planes, no alerts. It was an atmosphere we had been seeking for a long time. On the other side of the fence the locals were stopping to look at us.

In the middle of the night, the train started again. We didn't know what the next stop would be. We passed a city unknown to us. We were told that this was Duvivier. After a while we realized that the train was running in the opposite direction. Then we stopped in Duvivier station. We spent two hours there until we finally left again for an unknown destination.

My father took this opportunity to describe to us the beauty of both the Algerian landscape and the city of Algiers that he knew well. I believe that he just wanted to distract us from thinking of the war and give us something to look forward to. He described the cloudless azure sky, the dependable daily sunshine, the white houses, and the generously wide avenues, the narrow cobblestone streets of the Kasbah, which were the joy of the tourists, the deep blue sea, and the splendid night sky, full of stars. I felt hopeful. I would finally have my vacation on the beaches of Algiers and would watch the sun go down into the Mediterranean, just as though I were at Hammam-Lif on the Tunisian coast. And I would know the soft summer nights, so favored by lovers.

Early the following morning, the train stopped in a small village buried in the heart of tremendous mountains. Someone in our group recognized the area and told us we were back in Ghardimaou, Tunisia, a village bordering on Algeria. The stationmaster, flanked by a policeman announced that he had received orders to send us back to Béja. There was apparently no way for us to stay in Ghardimaou or in Algeria, since some of us might be in the incubation period and could start an epidemic. Hearing these words sent us into a cold sweat. How could anyone send us back to the very killing fields and to the inferno of daily bombing from which we had tried so valiantly to escape? Didn't that mean going back to the anguish of continuous alerts and bomb-dropping airplanes? This unbearable state of affairs had to be avoided at all cost.

My father, always very astute and quick in his decisions, managed to get us out of the station by paying off one of the convoy guards. We found ourselves in Ghardimaou, where the inhabitants were primarily Arabs who spoke fairly good French. On the village square there were stores filled with food, drinks, and many other items that we had not seen in a very long time. Surrounding the square were mulberry trees that created an ideal setting for café owners. Oblivious of the few drivers using the square, they would install their tables and chairs underneath this natural umbrella. More mulberry trees bordered the neighboring streets, and the sight of them brought me back to the schooldays when our teachers encouraged us to breed silkworms. That was one way for us to get a good grade and also to have fun. We used to put the cocoons in a pile. That was the time when we also put clothing and blankets in a pile, to be given to Belgian or Dutch refugees whose countries had been invaded by the Germans. My father, who was called up as a reservist to the French army in 1939, and was acquainted with the administration, was skeptical about the success of such enterprises.

At that time, when my father came home on leave, I was happy to see him. His military uniform made a strong impression on me, and made me feel proud of him. I loved to put on his khaki cap. Although I had no understanding of the army, as I didn't know what military service entailed, I was proud to see him in uniform, which reminded me of the army songs we had learned in school. Our teacher used to tell us that in wartime we had to fight to defend our homeland. She would talk to us about the heroic deeds of Maréchal Pétain, the great savior of the country, although I am sure she had never seen war. The irony of history shows us heroes becoming traitors and traitors becoming heroes. It all depends on the circumstances. And life continues and people do not change. In other places, governors became the governed, landlords the workers, and workers the managers. We want to change something, but in the end we change only the roles. But the men who play these roles will never change. They will remain the same, with their constructive and destructive inclinations.

Here in Ghardimaou a new life was about to start, one filled with hope. We had run away from our beautiful city and its surroundings in our desperate attempt to escape the war. But we could not run away from the dreadful typhus whose bacillus we carried within us.

A new life full of hope? Yes, but only for the first day. The next day, my mother and I developed a fever. My father, who when placed in an unpleasant situation generally denied it and pretended that it did not exist, tried to reassure us by saying, "It's nothing serious." But the family was large and feeling responsible for all of us, he could not avoid linking the fever to typhus. It would have been very dangerous to allow ourselves to be caught by the local authorities who were strictly following the orders they received. They generally abandoned questionably sick people to tents away from the cities, and although doctors were sent to them for regular checkups, the efforts were usually useless. People continued to die every day and burials followed one another. Luckily my father was not stubborn and decided that we should somehow take to the road once again.

It just so happened that he ran into an Arab man from Béja, whose family he knew well. After a cup of coffee together, my father found out that this man was actually in the medical field and that he knew a lot about what was going on with the epidemic. When my father told him confidentially about my mother, without even knowing exactly what my mother's condition was, he said to my father that he was not sure what she had, but that the authorities would certainly suspect her of having typhus. He advised my father not to approach anyone on this subject and to go somewhere where there was no medical authority. My father was very happy to have found this man and asked him where he suggested we should go. The Arab man, whose name I don't remember, took a piece of paper and quickly drew a sketch with directions how to get to a safe place, where there were caves in the high mountains. My father did not lose a minute before starting on our new journey, and he said that we had to go fast because nightfall was imminent and we could miss our path.

TYPHUS

Once again we were walking, but this time with a better sense of destination.

"Our destiny seems to be clearer now," said my father reassuringly.

"Yes," responded my mother sarcastically, "we are going to meet life or maybe death." My father didn't like my mother's remark. But he continued his walk without replying.

For security reasons, my father led us through fields and along smaller and larger brooks that we then had to cross. Exhausted, and with great difficulty, we followed him, changing direction several times. Night started to dim the daylight. We had to find a shelter for the night. My father found a cave at the foot of a mountain. Looking at the sketch, he said, "This is the right place. We will spend the coming days and maybe months here." My mother looked exhausted from the walk holding my baby brother.

One could not wish for a safer shelter, tucked away from all external danger. However, dangers also attack from within. It was only days before six of us were hit by typhus. Somehow, my father, my sister Judith and my younger brother had been spared.

Judith had cleaned the cave in order to spread our blankets and rugs that we had been carrying all along. For the first time we felt relaxed to be relieved of their weight.

Our refuge was surrounded by peaks of the beautiful Atlas chain and no one could see us from a distance. This was quite reassuring. Outside the cave, deep furrows dug by the metal belts of British tanks had filled up with water, tadpoles and toads. The only food we had left was sugar and Judith decided to make sugared water. Using a towel, she filtered the water contained in the furrows. She then added the sugar to our single mug, and from this we each drank, one after the other.

The next morning, as we woke up, we noticed a man looking around, not far from our cave. We had never seen this man before. My father's friend from our town had been kind enough not only to give us directions to the refuge but also to provide a guard for our security and daily needs. The man had a note written on a small piece of paper explaining to my father that he would be our guard and that he would be of service to us for as long as we needed him. Furthermore he mentioned that there would be no charge for the service, it was with compliments from our fellow Béja citizen.

The man was an honest guard. He came every morning and stayed at the entrance of the cave without saying a word. My father used him for all kinds of errands. In the evening he would leave us, but not before closing the entrance with

British fuel cans which he stacked one on top of the other. Then he covered all these cans with branches so no one could see the cave. He was the only one who knew where the cave was.

Although we spent forty days living like vagrants, we experienced them as a peaceful interlude, protected from bombing and fear, but also far away from other people. We were very weak and could hardly move. Our heartbeats were the only sign that we were still alive, and they helped us to hold on despite the cold, the hunger, and the illness. We survived thanks to my father's love and to Judith's sugared water.

My father had manifold duties; he served as head of the family, mother, doctor and guard of the entrance to the cave. He realized that the condition of his wife and children was slowly deteriorating. We were more dead than alive, but he preferred to see us die together rather than abandoned in a camp. He certainly would dig our graves and sing hymns for our dead. He had overcome fear and despair and was clinging to hope, which increased with the passing of time.

Outside there was a mixture of heavy rains, strong winds, and sunshine that dried up the landscape but brought us some welcome warmth. We had been entombed in the dark and cold of that cave for so long. From time to time the baby would cry for milk and his mother's soft touch. How had we survived, as we did, on only sugared water? It was a miracle. Silence spread over us, occasionally broken by a gust of wind, a silence likely to become eternal.

Days went by, and my father, helpless against the forces of nature, was waiting for the verdict. Our bodies, ridden with disease, had not much vitality left in them. The very same bodies that had been cherished and cajoled by the warmth of a mother, a grandmother, or a loving relative were now being kept alive only by the heat of the fever. Soon, even my father got sick and fell unconscious. Judith, who was only twelve, took charge of the situation. She revealed herself to be full of courage, dedication and love. She was like a mother, working tirelessly and selflessly. She was a wonderful nurse. Believing she was impervious to the disease, she took care of us all with love, reassuring each of us, always smiling, despite her state of near exhaustion.

My father had been the last to fall ill, and the last to recover. But ultimately, we all received God's favorable verdict—we were going to live. Judith, who never got sick herself, had managed to save the family, her only possession.

Before taking the train back to our town, we wanted to spend the last day visiting our faithful guard and thank him for his honest devotion. My father brought along a bag full of food that he had bought at the market, and some money. It took us over an hour to reach his dwelling high up in the mountains, where he lived in a simple hut. For the first time since our illness we were happy to breathe the fresh air of the mountains. While my father was talking with the guard, his wife prepared fresh flat bread for us. We played with his children outside. Then we walked back to our cave to spend the last night there before our return.

The Germans had been pushed back from the south by the 8th British army which came from Libya after defeating the Germans and from the north by the Americans. Bizerte, the last German-occupied stronghold, had not yet given up, but we could clearly hear church bells ringing out for victory. Heading back to our hometown, under conditions far more precarious than when we had left, ruins were all that we encountered—everywhere. Within the town, a few houses had been left more or less intact—except for the doors and windows, which had evidently been used by the soldiers to make fires during the winter. We settled in one of these houses and slowly began the process of trying to lead a normal life.

We had grieved over our vanished childhood; but it had not really been lost. We had been given the chance to regain it. A new life was spread out before us, and we only had to learn some new steps on heretofore unfamiliar paths. We had been spared by the ultimate "Judge", as we had overcome fear, bombings, disease, hunger, and brutal weather. We had survived through difficult times, and we had not lost hope and trust in life. I am sure my grandmother would have cried in her tomb. I felt a strong drive for life, ready to walk in the drenching rain or in the burning sun. I would never forget the familiar faces of Fatma, my teacher Mr. Vilmai, the German pilot, and Dr. Cohen. I would always keep in my heart the memory of the priest, the rabbi and the imam, whom I had known at a young age, the carter, who took a few members of our family on his cart, the old man, the owner of the donkeys, who alleviated our burden by letting us use his donkeys to carry our bags, the French stationmaster, who enabled us to move forward on our journey and all the people who lent a hand and made our life less burdensome. I extend my thanks to all the people I had known during my childhood. I would respect everyone, without regard for his or her religion, race and culture. I would love all faces I knew and I would get to know. Above all, I would never forget the "Judge", who gave us life again in that isolated cave, in the middle of nature.

The Germans chose our country as a battleground. They killed innocent people to gain glory. But that was a sign of spiritual weakness on their part. They turned their own country into a battlefield and their palaces into ruins. Their heroes are lying underground. Their women became widows, and their children orphans. That is the fate of any dictatorship. The strong tend to crush the weak, but in the end, the weak remain the strongest. Any immoral deed creates strong reactions that become destructive to the perpetrator himself. In fact, weakness attracts evil, but it is limited in time. Sooner or later the roles are reversed.

Life goes on; fair weather follows the storm; day follows night. Nature is made up of opposites: right and wrong, north and south, positive and negative, good and evil, beauty and ugliness, happiness and misery, love and hate. But people are naive. They always swing from one extreme to the other. They do not understand the basic rule of balance, which frankly is quite an art. The underlying causes of imbalance have to be detected. Nature has been created to exist in harmony. The whole universe is based on a balance of forces. We use the word evil, whereas evil exists neither in nature nor in humans. What we face are divergent forces and different elements. Contingent upon the manner in which these forces and elements are used, the results will be good or bad. It is for us to know how to work with what we have to produce good and constructive outcomes. Those who do not understand the characteristics of these forces and elements should stay away from them.

We can use atomic energy to destroy people, but also to cure disease. Venom can kill but can also be the basis of remedies. Whether we avoid or create evil is a matter of degree. But if we create evil, we must take full responsibility for it. Those who understood the basic rules were able to create goodness, beauty, music, literature and many of the other joys that touch our senses. Through positive work we can experience a feeling of satisfaction which is nothing other than the mixture of love and goodness filling us with its blessings. It is often difficult to describe these sweet sensations. These are forces that come from afar, to unite with us and wake the sleeping being in us.

There is no joy in this world that comes close to these feelings of goodness and love which reverberate their beneficial influence upon those close to us. The sight of a person beaming with joy, happiness, goodness and love, immediately takes one in. It is in our power to belong to that category of persons.

On the other hand, we will always encounter people who do not find us pleasant or lovable; no need to retaliate and become hateful toward them. Hatred can only be destructive. Let us ignore hostile comments and avoid provoking such persons, particularly if we wish to remain the way we are. They do not even think about what they say.

War is a sign of imbalance. It is not through force that one re-establishes the balance. History teaches us that the deployment of force has never led to a durable peace. Above all, let us respect each other. No nation is superior to another. This is also true of religions and cultures. A victory does not mean peace; it only brings a temporary period of quiet. It is a grave error to underestimate someone smaller. The greatness of a nation or a country is not measured by the number of its citizens or the size of its territory. Let's not rejoice in our victories. No one is invincible. A long period of peace offers no guarantees for the future. We need to remain wary of the patience of those looking for revenge. Time does not matter in history, and history is only an episode in the life of the human race.

EMILE TUBIANA

The author on the balcony of his "new house" during a short visit to Béja in 1992.

The Béja train station

RETURNING TO OUR TOWN

Our new house was located near the station, and the railroad tracks ran parallel to our bedroom walls. Needless to say our nights were not very quiet. Freight trains were the only ones allowed to run; they carried American soldiers to the battle area of Bizerte, where the Germans had lost ground but were still holding this port as the last symbol of domination over their enemies.

The inhabitants of Béja who had fled during the bombing were gradually returning to their city. People were entitled or took for themselves the right to live in abandoned houses, or whatever was left of them. Eventually a relatively normal life set in again. The stores reopened, although they did not have anything to sell. Meanwhile the British soldiers cleared the ruins, retrieving from the debris corpses impossible to identify. A foul smell spread over the whole city. Streets were strewn with debris, furniture, doors and broken windows, but not for long—since anyone could grab a piece of wood to fill up an opening in a house or shelter, or use it to make a semblance of a door or a window frame. No thought was given to appearance or color, as long as the lumber could serve a purpose.

Ration tickets appeared. Béja got food through the American military trains. In order to get a piece of bread, one had to stand on very long lines every day. My father found a solution to this problem. He made an agreement with the baker who gave us fresh bread; in return for our bread, my father made shoes for his large family.

On the whole, food was insufficient, we were malnourished. My father loathed the idea of a black market; as for me, I saw nothing wrong with it. The local authorities could not supply our needs, while the

Americans enjoyed a surplus of goods. It could not hurt them if one were to think of taking a small portion away from them, I reasoned. I thought it was rather silly to pass up such an opportunity, considering the dire conditions under which we lived and the need of the Americans for fresh food. Therefore I decided to make a deal with them. I enjoyed my barter business but kept it secret from my father, only my mother knew. My idea was simple, but people had to trust me. French people were the only ones to receive stamps for wine. They were lacking food and they were eager to exchange their wine stamps for the promise of getting American army food. They gave me their stamps for wine. In exchange I supplied them what they needed, for which they paid me. Luckily, Béja was the last stop for all trains carrying Americans to Bizerte, the biggest battlefront. That made it easy for me to barter the wine and obtain food, clothing, blankets and even dollars—

a currency that I was seeing for the first time in my life.

My business became so successful that I soon needed a place to store all the goods I was accumulating. I made arrangements with a middle aged woman, whose husband had been drafted in the French army. She was alone and did not have any income. Before the war, this warehouse was the warehouse of the French Saint-Frère Company, which her husband managed. The warehouse was full of empty wheat bags. I had them all stacked in one corner. In exchange for its use, I gave her chocolate, cookies, canned food, or anything I had. The deal was concluded; she had the keys of the warehouse, and was free to enter and to take whatever she desired for her own consumption. She could not take any goods for resale.

Soldiers soon found out about this warehouse, and every day they would line up, exchanging their belongings for eggs and wine. As soon as the trains were gone, the inhabitants of Béja would come to pick-up fresh supplies.

Eventually the police discovered my business, searched the premises and took over my warehouse. I was furious! I could not find any justification for their behavior. Why did they prohibit me from making my deals? I was not hurting anybody. Quite the contrary, I was of help to the refugees who could not find anything anywhere else, neither food nor clothing. In addition, wine was very important to the soldiers who went to the front, just as important as food for those who were lacking it. My prices even varied according to the financial means of the individual customer. The poor, for example, were not expected to pay for anything. Therefore I was furious, but I did not panic—being somehow confident that the situation would resolve itself. After all, the American colonel in charge of the movement of the American soldiers who were going to the front where battles with the Germans were still going on, appreciated my services. Every day, reinforcement troops arriving from Algeria were passing through our town and stopping for resupply if needed.

I visited the colonel in a freight car that he used as an office. I was in tears when I told him the whole story. He listened to me very carefully and tried to calm me down by assuring me that everything would turn out all right. He then called ten soldiers and ordered them to go and free my warehouse—an action that went far beyond my greatest hopes. I had stopped crying, and I followed the ten soldiers. I was certainly well on the way to getting back my belongings. However, things were to become rough. The soldiers did not bother to give any warning or explanation to the policemen guarding the warehouse. They simply grabbed them by the neck and pushed them out, ordering them to leave me in peace. The policemen complied sheepishly but threatened to take their revenge as soon as the Americans were gone.

The colonel had taken a liking to me, and sometimes we would spend hours together. His help exceeded my expectations. I even had two soldiers standing guard at the entrance to my warehouse. They put up a sign stating "Property of the US ARMY", and this allowed me to work without worries.

Being prosperous in my work did not make me selfish—not at all. I really felt for these soldiers who went to the front to fight for our freedom. I respected and admired their logic and their love for justice. And no sooner had the train left the station than I found myself praying for them. But in the evening, trains would return filled with wounded soldiers, and that made me sad. I would recognize faces that I had seen a few days earlier. With all my heart, I offered them free wine or fresh water that I carried from a public fountain. I recognized the voices of some of the soldiers whose faces were covered with bloody bandages. Although the station was guarded, I could walk in and out freely—which made the stationmaster envious of my privileges. All the soldiers knew me. I also gave them coats and capes made from blankets I had received from them in exchange for wine.

Unfortunately there were many faces I did not see again. When I asked about them I was answered with silence. Some had the courage to tell me that their friend didn't make it. I was the first to know about these poor soldiers who had come here to die, far away from their loved ones. Their mothers, their fathers, and maybe their wives would receive the news much later, maybe in a month or two. I am sure that not knowing what was going on in the war was very hard for them. Of course, the newsreels were mainly showing the victory part of the war. Some feel their loss by instinct and some do not feel it. I was imagining with pain the parents and the entire family crying when the officer knocked at the door to announce the bad news. These scenes alone made me sad and I cried without seeing them. This goes for the American, the British, and the Commonwealth soldiers who died on our land without the warmth of the presence of any family member. I felt the same way for the enemy soldiers, be they Germans or Italians, be they from Asia or any other countries. I was convinced that they would have preferred staying in their country and enjoying life. Unfortunately, many factors contributed to their recruitment, be it peer pressure, propaganda, the draft, or the media.

All go to war to die for their homeland; at least that's what they're led to believe.

Bizerte was finally liberated. But the railroad traffic had not slowed down. Soldiers were now going to Italy to fight, but they were still traveling through Bizerte. We would get the news over the radio, or by way of the wounded soldiers who came back to us. Numerous trains carried Italian prisoners; they seemed to be happy that the fighting was over for them.

Italians do not like fighting, according to my appreciation at that time. For many centuries, the Mediterranean has had a beneficial influence on its surrounding nations by imbuing them with peaceful feelings. The long reign of the Greeks and Romans belonged to an ancient past, during which that sea was tormented. But these warriors have disappeared, leaving a Mediterranean that is calm once again. Blessed with sunshine all through the year, the sea appears serene—with its soft waves, sweet winds and fragrant scents.

The martial spirit prevalent among the Middle Eastern nations hardly matches the symbol of the Mediterranean—it will not endure—the Blue Sea will again serve as a link between its coasts that hold such a variety of nations, with their different political and religious backgrounds. This Blue Sea cannot be denied. Visitors, when they first come upon her, are seduced by the atmosphere of love and generosity that she generates. After all, she nurtures people. One cannot resist her charm and beauty; her golden, finely-sanded beaches are universally appreciated. One feels transported into another world. Germans, Americans and British have also had contact with all her benign qualities, but sadly under unfortunate circumstances. Even France gave up in the face of Tunisia's peaceful spirit, where the women have no other ambition than to cherish their children, nourish them and wrap them in their love and the warmth of their heart.

Any nation with a propensity for war, upon discovering the Mediterranean for the first time, is fated to lay down its arms, and irresistibly bewitched by her will contribute to maintaining her charm. At that time, for example, Tunisia had a remarkable diversity in its population; Tunisians and Europeans were living in peace and harmony generated by the influence of the Mediterranean Sea.

Because of the wartime environment, the black market in Béja had become a free market. The police followed the movement and had become my customers. At City Hall, where the news were posted, one could follow the daily moves at the front by the position of a straight wire stretched out on geographical maps. The city was filled with soldiers. I loved to talk with them. The Americans, who introduced me to their country, liked to show me pictures of their spouse, their children or their fiancée. Their words conveyed a mixture of enthusiasm and nostalgia. They shared with me their plans for a happy future. The colonel was from Pennsylvania, and a nice guy from Long Island gave me his Chase Manhattan bank card and his safe keys before he went to Bizerte. His colleague who was wounded returned and told me the bad news about his friend. In this way a warm bond had been created between the soldiers and me. It was sad to think that by order of their government the poor soldiers had to be expatriated and fight abroad, leaving behind what was dearest to them and that they were uncertain whether they would ever see their country and their loved ones again.

I developed a similar relationship with the Italian and German soldiers who, although they were held prisoners in the mill located near the station, had the freedom to walk around among the Americans and the inhabitants in the evenings. I was not at all shocked by this mingling of soldiers who were actually enemies. They did not differ much in their way of thinking. They shared the hope of seeing the end of the war, so that they would be able to go back home again to their families. I realized that there was no difference in the looks and the behavior of both the victorious and the defeated. They all wanted peace and the chance to lead a normal life. They realized that by killing the enemy they were killing members of their own human species and, by the same token, were killing themselves. They all revered the same God, ignoring the fact that God does not take part in the atrocities and the destructive acts committed by men.

On Sunday mornings, Americans, British, Germans, Italians and French attended the same service in our church. They all sang the same hymns, in different languages. They felt like brothers and were convinced of the stupidity of war and of the moral suffering it brings about. Only such men are able to draw the conclusions of fruitless warfare. Only these men can remember that they shared common thoughts and hopes. Only such men can build a new world in which the human race will live in peace.

The Germans taught me how to play the harmonica. I discovered the song "Lili Marlene" for the first time, and I found it soft and soothing. To its melody, I visualized huge green forests in Germany and tall blonde women with blue or green eyes.

My strongest wish then was to some day visit all the homelands of the different soldiers—since each of them praised his own as the most beautiful.

Some of our inhabitants behaved hatefully to the Germans, whom they called *les boches* (bosh). I disapproved of my fellow citizens, since I believed in loving my neighbor, and banishing hatred. In my eyes, apart from their language and uniform, these soldiers were not different from each other.

EMILE TUBIANA

"THEIR NAME LIVETH FOR EVERMORE"

American Military Cemetery

I witnessed what you did, you were fighters, you were charitable, and noble. You gave your life to save ours. You will never be forgotten and I thank you very much. In turn I shall recognize you and your children in all Americans. God Bless America and its children.

Commonwealth Military Cemetery

*To all who lost their life fighting the enemies of freedom,
I am honored to tell you:
I do not forget the day you came down from the sky.
Many of us watched the "balloons"
as we called the parachutes.
I was with you the day the German planes bombed us.
You gave me courage and candy.
As I lost conscience, the candy revived me and saved my life.
I thank you and God bless your souls.
You are forever our beloved friends and saviors.*

L'hôtel de ville—Béja City Hall

THE LIBERATED ZONES

Balls were organized for the benefit of the liberated zones. All the soldiers in town attended. The most impressive and grandiose ball was the one which commemorated the landing in France. It was clear that the war would end soon and the thought of this filled us with happiness. We could almost touch the peace around us. Sorrow, anxiety and fear were gradually disappearing, making room for joy and happiness, and each day was filled with shining rays of sun that warmed our hearts. We rediscovered our zest for life and appreciated once more our cherished freedom.

Before the war, we were similar to herds of cattle, indifferent to life. It was only with the cessation of the fighting that we were able to appreciate the precious beauty of life. Actually it was because of the war that we acquired a lust for life—for all the needs that life requires us to fill in terms of food, work and sleep—and we appreciated the simple evenings spent on our peaceful doorstep. We talked and told stories, while lovers hid in dark corners, protected by the complicity of the night. But in this new life we felt some emptiness, created by the loss of relatives or friends. We tried to go on as if nothing had happened, but it was very hard not to remember those we loved. They were part of the familiar scene of our town and we could not forget their faces, their voices, their personalities and their participation in the life of the community. Despite our joy of having survived the atrocities of the war, we were reminded of them each time we stumbled over the ruins still congesting our streets. How could we forget them when we came across their widows and children? The new military cemeteries, the American, the British, the German, and the Italian became a constant reminder of the war. We might forgive, but could we really forget?

Everything has changed, and this change is the prelude to a new era that has already transformed our universe and will therefore present us with distressing events, an era of mistrust. The powerful nations will go the way of force, using as their motto *si vis pacem, para bellum* (if you want peace, prepare for war). They will submit to technology and science, at the detriment of such values as faith and love. We will see the beginning of an age of doubt which may never end. Nations will see their people uprooted and living in exile, away from their loved ones, and suffering from nostalgia.

Is it really necessary to invite still more wars and atrocities in order to appease minds overheated with their ideals—democracy, socialism or communism? Can an ideology be based on anarchy, terrorism, destruction or disorder? Must we go to these extremes, ending up with innocent victims on our conscience? A bomb may be more dramatic than a human voice, but the relentless human voice will not surrender and will defend its cause.

Examine what happened to past civilizations, to the cultural treasures of humanity; they were all destroyed by force. Are there no other ways to solve our problems? The heads of government maintain that they represent public opinion. Is this a hoax used to deny their responsibility? Public opinion has not really been expressed. Even the press cannot be relied upon, inasmuch as journalists are not totally unbiased in reporting material. There will always be leaders guiding the nations through various means.

Perhaps it would serve us better to ask the opinions of children. After all, they are pure and untainted, unaware of the meaning of intrigue and lies. Their minds are healthy and free of unnecessary clutter, and they certainly are well qualified to give us honest answers to all the questions we could ask them.

Aren't there enough victims through natural disasters—earthquakes, floods, tornados, accidents, hunger, epidemics? Do we have to go to war to see our wealth disappear, which could be the base for all nations' happiness? Man is a slave to his weakness. He does not recognize when an evil is consuming him and, instead of getting rid of it, he allows himself to be destroyed.

Men are driven to slaughter in the name of freedom, independence, and homeland. Do they even understand the kind of freedom for which they are ready to give up their lives? What is the real meaning of that word freedom? What *freedom* do we see in the chains of our pride and hostility—the freedom to be hungry and feel miserable? Why talk about freedom from our chains?

Men are prisoners of their anatomy and deficiencies, of their traditions, of the education they have received and of the society in which they live.

It is senseless to die for freedom; actually, we must live for it. Let us rejoice in freedom, but more so in a freedom of the spirit. This is a positive strength that helps us with our actions in our professional, social and personal environments. And it is thanks to this strength that we achieve freedom—and attain love. It is far easier to love one's neighbor than to fight him.

We speak freely of the feeling we call love but do we understand it? Love is different from sex and beautiful women. It is a beauty that dwells within each of us, and it is our responsibility to discover it. Beautiful things need to be pursued if we wish to discover them. In the case of flowers we can reach their colorful loveliness only by pulling up the weeds that strangle them and obscure them from our view. Numerous treasures are buried in the earth, and we need to dig them up before we can enjoy them.

We know that we are surrounded by all kinds of forces. They too are waiting for us to uncover them so that we can then use them. There are also forces hidden inside us. It is through love and work that we can get in touch with them. Such forces are not the privilege of a social class, or of a nation. A woodcutter, a shoemaker or a homemaker may very well be endowed with more of these forces than some world-famous personality. More than one Einstein or Pasteur is probably hidden somewhere among us! People are often unaware of their potential, and they need an outside event or effort to release it.

Could we really take seriously a new Leonardo da Vinci or a new Jesus? People would prefer to select a new car model if given a choice between a Madame Curie and an automobile.

Each of us carries from birth a range of potential, from kindness and love to disease, and from great intelligence to sheer stupidity. It is in our power to actualize some of this potential. This realization depends upon our lifestyle and our daily actions. The laws of nature that we keep discovering are not eternal. They become valuable only to the extent that our knowledge increases. As a consequence, these laws can be extremely variable. Each evil may well have its remedy, but one must understand it well in order to heal it. The same principle holds true for nature, which encompasses divergent forces. Once they are understood, they can be used appropriately. The education we have received is far from adequate, because we are manipulating the wrong tools with it. It is not always the "good" which brings us pleasure, or the "evil" which saddens us. Feelings provoked by grief or melancholy, joy or pleasure, help us discover the true meaning of *good* and *evil*.

It is difficult to decide wisely, to

recognize good feelings or real friends. Only the trial and error testing we undergo justifies our choices. It is as a result of such testing that we can make our best decisions. All we need is a little something—a wind, a storm, a tune, a landscape, a certain ambiance, a feeling of danger, or meeting a particular person—in order for us to find the right path. We can then make our own choice. The absence of any sense of remorse as well as our clear conscience confirm to us that we made the right decision.

Justice is not the privilege of judges, priests, or rabbis. Physicists, biologists or high-ranking university officials do not hold the secrets of science. Some of them may be competent, and others may not. But society knows how to choose according to the rules we have just described. Even as air and wind, the true and the false, or truth and falsehood, do not have any limits. Let us not give away our freedom of choice, freedom of expression and thus abdicate our destiny. If need be, let us neutralize our selfishness and resist our pride. Our duty towards ourselves dictates that we admit to our shortcomings, weaknesses and errors. It is never too late to change direction, or to review our decisions and modify them. Would it be wise to cross the desert with a sick camel? There is too much at stake. This holds true also when we realize that our choices and decisions do not rest on a solid foundation.

Any work which has been started must be finished under the best conditions. A piece of land must be plowed before one can sow; then one must attend to it and wait faithfully for its fruit. In the same fashion, a mother-to-be is indirectly taking care of her baby by taking good care of herself. She will then be able to wait full of confidence, knowing that everything will be all right. Each event has its time, and there is a special time for everything. There are, of course, unpredictable and unforeseeable events. That is why one must be careful, attentive and perceptive.

A good watchman does not allow himself to sleep; he is always on alert. We have an obligation to fulfill our responsibilities, however unimportant they may seem. No matter how easy or how difficult our work may be, it involves a high degree of accountability, dictated by our conscience. Money assumes a secondary role; our aptitude will become clearly apparent through our fruitful work.

EMILE TUBIANA

Elementary and boarding school, Béja

CHILDHOOD REGAINED

BACK TO SCHOOL

When school reopened, there were still reminders of war surrounding us. On our way there streets were blocked with the ruins of fallen buildings. Oddly enough, the school building was almost intact. The desks were in order in the classrooms, as though nothing had happened. In the beginning there were only a few students, since some of our schoolmates had disappeared. Others were still on the farms where their families had sought shelter. Among our teachers, some new faces had replaced some familiar ones. Between the half-empty classrooms and the new teachers, a rather somber ambiance reigned. We did not feel comfortable. Under the understanding eye of our teachers, we spent the first day telling each other our stories—where we had been, what we had done, what had happened to us. Every one of us had lived through a different experience, some had suffered a great deal, and others had lost relatives. The luckiest ones had managed to seek refuge in Algeria, right at the start of the war. They brought back with them fond memories, as if they had just returned from a vacation. They had had a pleasant journey, attended good schools, either in Algiers or in Constantine, and had spent most of their time on sunny beaches. They had not suffered from malnutrition, since their food had not been rationed; they had been housed in refugee camps but under the best conditions.

Since we were at a tender age, when jealousy is not well controlled, we polarized instinctively into two camps. In one were the youngsters who had suffered through the war, and in the other, those who had not been touched by it. It took months for this grudge to disappear, and for the groups to finally develop into a large, cohesive whole.

Our new teacher, who replaced Mr. Vilmai, had a foot injury—a result of his fighting in the war—which had caused him to be discharged from the army. Instantly, we cared for him, since we realized that he was one of us and that he had suffered just as we had; and what is more, he was very sweet and compassionate. He showed interest in our recent misery and tried to give us moral support. He particularly cared for Maurice, whose father had died. This role was not an easy one for him to assume, since he needed comfort just as much as we did.

As life returned to normal, I had to curtail my business with the Americans and focus on my studies. But after all that we had gone through, I experienced great difficulty staying interested in school. We were no longer children. The events we had faced had left their marks on us and were engraved in our memory. I no longer felt the urge to learn nor did any of my friends. Who cared whether or not Louis XIV was a good king! History mattered little to us. Our own experience had become our central focus, and we ourselves had turned into kings in our own way. Our teacher understood our state of mind and, as a result, was patient with us. He realized that our young age did not match our experience, and that we could not behave as we had prior to the war.

Every train arrival stirred up buried feelings. I felt much closer to the Americans than I did to my fellow countrymen. I found myself hanging around the train station rather than going to school. The only drawback was that my parents had to write notes to excuse my absences. It was not our fault that we were seeking freedom after everything we had seen. Wasn't it up to us to excuse and forgive the adults for having put us in unbearable situations where suffering was the primary reality? I no longer accepted this authority and refused to submit myself to it. I felt like a grown-up, able to take responsibility for myself. I decided to write my own notes of excuse and to forge my innocent father's signature. I was fully aware of the danger of my action, but as a minor I was not at risk. I was drawn by the thirst for freedom and independence, and I was not the only one to follow this drive. The idea of punishment did not frighten me, since that punishment would seem mild in comparison with what we had gone through.

Nonetheless, the teachers were required to enforce the rules, and they had to demand this note of excuse to protect themselves. Of course we could not fool them and they recognized the forgery, but as long as they had a signed note they were safe. In this manner lies and superficiality returned to everyday life, and I did not feel any guilt.

Grown-ups, in silent collusion, pretended not to know any of this in order to safeguard what they considered to be their just authority. I was against neither well-deserved authority nor justified power, but those who exercised them had to take into account our state of mind and be more flexible. Our equilibrium had been destroyed; suffering, be it physical or emotional, requires time and patience to heal. It was the responsibility of our elders to behave in a certain gentle and subtle way, in order to bring us back into balance. They needed to act lovingly toward us, to instill in us love for our surroundings. It was essential that we be treated with care, understanding and serenity if we were ever to develop a new taste for school and for work.

Laws must not be imperative and absolute, but rather take into consideration the details of a particular case. It would be simplistic to attempt to cure all diseases with the same medicine. Any given problem has its solutions; the difficulty lies in truly identifying the problem. The doctor has to give his diagnosis before prescribing a remedy.

In the teaching field, an educator must possess the qualities appropriate for his profession. His attitude cannot be the same with every student; his role is to discover the various problems within each of them. With this knowledge, he can re-establish the peace of mind which was lost through war or other circumstances. In any case, that attitude rescues a child and generates a stream of confidence and friendship that flows between teacher and student.

By deciding that any one thing is forbidden, not only are old problems going unsolved but new ones are being compounded. Authority can only expect respect if that respect is deserved. The era of Caesars is over. We must do away with blind discipline and rules which have no place in a modern society; certainly not in one that seeks independence and is hostile to revolution, disorder, theft, and crime.

When children go astray, we must find the cause among their parents, their educators and society at large. It is essential to know how to create a balance between the state of mind and moral support. Those who do not have the capacity to fulfill such a role must step down from their hierarchical position.

The Béja post office reopened after the war.

THE END OF THE AMERICAN PRESENCE

The Americans left for good, and daily life seemed to resume its normal course. I missed my American friends, however, and would go to see all their movies. This was exactly what I did on the eve of a very important examination for the *Certificat d'études*—the French completion certificate once given to 11–14 year-olds. Evidently it was not a wise move, since I should have spent time at home studying the material. The following day, my teacher came up to me and expressed her disapproval of my behavior. How she found out about my going out remains a mystery to me! She was disappointed in me since she had placed her utmost confidence in me and another schoolmate named Pierre. Pierre's choice, unlike my own, had been to spend days studying, putting any thoughts of distractions aside. My teacher was proud of him and considered Pierre the best example of her successful teaching. She finally told me not to sit for the certification exam, since I was bound to fail. As for myself, at that time, this diploma had no value whatsoever. Therefore, on this, the day of the exam, I found myself very relaxed. In fact, my teacher was quite right; how was I going to pass when I had not memorized anything? I could not learn anything by heart; that had always been my weak spot or maybe my strong one.

Toward the end of the afternoon, there was a big crowd in the schoolyard. Parents and candidates, as well as our teacher were waiting impatiently to see the posted results. Our teacher had assuredly come to congratulate Pierre, who was bound to pass. When the list was tacked in place, I saw my name but Pierre's name was not included.

Since then, I have understood the meaning of self-confidence. I am the type of person who never loses courage, and I never undertake anything without wanting to do it. I had taken this exam with confidence and the expectation of passing, but I would have accepted failure without regret or remorse. Sometimes failure has its positive side; it is one of life's challenges. My teacher had tried to discourage me but had not succeeded in taking away my own faith—which, in my innocent way became my strength. Nothing is more valuable than one's own experience. One has to master the tasks of life. Each of us needs to find his own way and to make decisions regarding his own life and destiny. We must assume responsibility for our mistakes rather than blame others for them. We must also realize that the advice we get is dictated by our passive behavior.

The lives of children are in the hands of adults who are not always capable of handling that responsibility, especially if they have not found their own direction. Since they are ostensibly mature, parents take possession of their children and make decisions for them concerning their future. As a matter of fact, their role should be very different. Parents should be preparing their children to become independent. It is actually detrimental to children when their parents attempt to hold on to them and stifle them with the kind of love that is a form of selfishness and a sign of the parent's inaptitude for the role of caregiver.

There is a form of love that is expressed in respect for freedom. Such love does not express itself with words and kisses, but through good thoughts and generous and disinterested actions. Such love is offered without reservation, limitation or expectation.

Such love is a moral wealth that obviates hatred and restores its true meaning to life. It allows us to appreciate goodness, beauty and perfection; it introduces us to joy, peace and security; it gives us faith, faith in believing.

Hammam-Lif with Mount Bou Kornine, and La Goulette

POSTWAR SUMMER VACATION

In June, after the examinations marking the end of the school term and before summer vacation, we enjoyed a relaxed rhythm. We still had to attend school, but we spent most of our time chatting. Our teacher told us little stories, commented on them and pointed out the moral. In the evening we would walk in small groups and look for girls our age; we would come across them, and that would be enough to boost our pride as pre-adolescents.

July was the starting point of our summer vacation. Soon we would separate and follow our parents to Hammam-Lif, La Goulette or even Saint-Germain or Radès. Some of us went to summer camp or to relatives in France.

Hammam-Lif and La Goulette are

two beaches located on opposite coasts along the Mediterranean, south-east and north-east of Tunis. In summertime there is a warm ambiance created by the charm of these cities when they are invaded by the inhabitants of Tunis, who are running away from the heat of the capital. Nights were enchanting and we would spend the greater part of our nights there on the beach, along with entire families—all searching for the coolness of a calm sea, without a wave.

I loved to stretch out on the fine sanded beach, staring endlessly at the purity of the sky lit up by millions of scintillating stars. My mind was empty and I was fascinated by that far-away world with which I had established some kind of link. I was absorbed by my universe and removed from the surrounding noises. I could no longer hear the calls of the ambulant vendors on the beach, praising their delicacies. The most remarkable evening was that of July 14th, Bastille Day, commemorating that day in 1789 which marked the end of the monarchy and celebrates the First French Republic. That night, shopkeepers had converted the beach into various areas: one for cooking, one for dancing, with Chinese lanterns, tables, and chairs; and another for the musicians. A crowd started to gather as soon as the sun went down. Some people lay down on the sand, and others sat at a table in one of the improvised restaurants, attracted by the smell of broiled food such as *meshwe*[1] or *merguez*[2]. Vendors were selling *briks*[3], *bonboloni*[4] and small bunches of jasmine stalks, whose strong perfume would mingle with the different aromas from hot dishes. The men wore jasmine behind their ears; as for the women, they adorned the low necklines of their blouses with it. At nine o'clock, fireworks were set off, culminating above the sea. A rare and colorful sight lit up the water, contrasting with the pure and starry sky. When the fireworks were over, the bands started to play—opening the way to frenetic and impatient young people. The girls had ensured that they would look more beautiful than ever, their suntanned complexions and dark eyes exerting a definite charm on the boys. The festivities continued until the wee hours, the following morning.

1. *meshwe:* meat broiled on a wood fire
2. *merguez:* hot spicy sausage
3. *brik:* A thin savory pastry filled with a mixture of meat and potatoes, and often egg, folded into a triangle and deep fried.
4. *bonboloni:* a round pastry similar to a doughnut

LIFE GOES ON

In September, autumnal breezes marked the end of our summer vacation—as well as the end of our carefree life. School benches were made ready to welcome us back. Our interlude of freedom was over, and a school year with discipline lay ahead of us. It was sad and hard to start school again. Wartime had been slowly, slowly erased from our memory; with the passing of time, wounds heal and the deepest painful feelings disappear. We were happy at the sight of our new French teacher, since she was very pretty; but soon her strictness made us forget her physical attractiveness. As for our Arabic teacher, a Muslim, he was overflowing with human kindness. Teaching for him was a game; he taught with humor and verve. He would tell us the stories of

"One Thousand and One Nights", which enchanted us. Our Arabic lessons were pure joy.

Strange as it may sound, we lived in Tunisia but were unaware of its culture and literature. Our teacher filled this void with knowledge, and thanks to him we discovered a beautiful language and a fascinating civilization from ancient times. We regretted that he was not respected by our French teachers, who believed to be the only upholders of the highest cultural values. Actually the French, who kept settling down in increasing numbers in Tunisia, either as farmers or in the administration, never seemed to recognize that a Tunisian was entitled to certain rights within his own homeland.

There were always some matters which put us in trouble with regard to our teacher. The question of unpolished shoes was one of them, and one that convinced me of the importance of the role each of us plays in our society. One morning, our teacher decided to focus on shoes and I was, of course, the first to be put on the spot.

"Have you looked at your shoes?"

"Yes, Madame."

"They are dirty. Did you polish them?"

"No, Madame."

I stiffened up when she asked me the reason for this oversight. As a punishment, I had to write one hundred times, "My shoes are dirty." And in order to confirm that statement, I decided to stop polishing my shoes—which elicited the same punishment. But I did not care. I was ahead of the game since I already had several sheets of paper filled with the line "My shoes are dirty." My classmates felt panicky each time our teacher inspected them. As for me, I would not budge, because I knew in what state my shoes were. My classmates would make the tips of their shoes shine by using either the back of their socks, their hand or their clean handkerchief. All that did not help; they were punished just as I was. But for them the punishment was not the end of the story, since they had to explain to their mother the dirt on their handkerchief. In my case I did not carry one. In my family there were always more children than the number of handkerchiefs at our disposal.

To tell the truth, I was not too proud of my stubbornness. What was the point of refusing to polish my shoes, and of having lines to write every day? Fortunately our teacher did not decide to use more drastic measures, such as asking me to bring a note from my parents. Therefore, one morning I decided to shine my shoes. My friends were going to be surprised and the teacher would be flabbergasted. Just the thought of it made me really happy! Unfortunately, man proposes and God disposes. The milkman was late, and my mother usually forbade my leaving the house without first having my coffee with milk. What I feared happened. After swallowing down my burning cup of coffee with milk, I ran to school, but I arrived late. While I was gently pushing the gate open, the principal saw me, called my name and took me to his office. He was lenient and just gave me a moral lecture. He was right, but was it my fault if the milkman was late? My argument was weak and I knew it. Time was moving along, and now I had to confront my teacher, this time with quite a substantial delay. She lashed out at me with a long list of reprimands, scolded me and sent me to the corner of the classroom, where I had to remain in a kneeling position, long after my friends had left school. In my mind I could visualize the stern interrogation of my father, wondering why I was so late returning home.

Within a few hours I had found myself in trouble with the principal, my teacher and my father. My mother would also have been on the list, if I had disobeyed her. And all this because of a milkman. He had put me in an embarrassing situation; moreover, he had deprived me of the pleasure I had anticipated because of my polished shoes.

I had to come to terms with reality, however; a milkman is important. By delivering his milk with a small delay, he had messed up my day and my hopes. I realized that this incident was part of daily life, of the little details that can have dramatic consequences. Small causes can engender large effects. Whether one man is indirectly responsible for it, the result remains the same. If a train is late, for one reason or another, its passengers, upon their arrival, will have to solve their problems. Some may be punished—or fired, in the case of an employee who has a tendency to be late. It is always embarrassing to enter a meeting after important decisions have already been made. The death or life of a person may depend upon the promptness of rescuers.

Examples can be multiplied at length. No one is spared, from people at the top level to people at the bottom of the ladder; and consequences can be serious.

We belong to a society in which, believe it or not, we all have a role to play. That role constitutes an indispensable part of the normal functioning of a community. Failure to assume one's role would mean creating a critical situation for oneself and for others. It is therefore imperative to fill this role conscientiously. I don't intend to preach an ideology, since an ideology would force us to follow a movement, to become enslaved and lose our individuality. It would deprive us of our freedom of thought, our freedom of expression and would perhaps become an obstacle on the path we have laid out for ourselves. However this path must not disturb our daily life, nor prevent us from doing our duty toward each other and society.

My problems with my teacher had

started from day one of the new school year. I was late that day and had refused to give an explanation. Had she understood that I was coming back to school against my will? She had become anxious and had asked me to go up to the blackboard with my vacation homework. I did not budge since I had nothing to tell her or to give her. Vacation is not a time to work; even less so, when one has successfully passed the *Certificat d'études*. I was gazing down, thinking of the good moments of the past summer. I was loath to look at the beauty of this woman which was spoiled by her aggressive behavior. Was it possible that such a pretty mouth could utter such virulent reproaches? Never mind, I did not pay much attention. She went on, admonishing other classmates who had forgotten to do their homework while on vacation. Most of them were petrified and stuttered their responses. By acting this way, they supposed they would gain her pity. Quite to contrary; she became more and more severe. I felt like rescuing my classmates, but decided to keep still since I could not hope for much in this situation.

Finally, the teacher went back to her desk, but only to pick on me once again. She called me to the board. At this point it was better to obey her. She gave me a piece of chalk and asked me to write down my memories of the vacation. Then I became furious inside myself. How dare she ask me to reveal to everyone what I treasured as my own personal possessions, my garden of secrets which I opened up from time to time for my own pleasure? The teacher stared at me. I did not move. To reveal my thoughts would have been insolent. I just lowered my head—when in fact, deep down I wanted to look straight into her beautiful dark eyes. I felt ridiculous, but what else could I do? She threw me out of the class and asked me to stand motionless in the schoolyard. It was obvious she wanted me to be noticed by the principal, who visited the classes in the morning. That is exactly what happened. The principal saw me, but did not pay much attention—evidently thinking I was on my way to the bathroom. Then I saw my friend Maurice, in tears, walking toward me. He too, had been expelled from the classroom. Had he not suffered enough during the war, in which his father had been killed? Did he also have to cry for such superficial reasons? I would have liked to have comforted him, but I did not dare. I even avoided looking at him. We were in the same schoolyard but separated from each other. I did not feel enough by myself to relive my vacation memories. Maurice's presence inhibited me and plunged me back in the atrocities of war, which I had thought were gone forever.

THE CONSCRIPTION OF TUNISIAN PEASANTS

When the war moved to Sicily and Italy, the French government needed soldiers to fight against the Italians and the Germans. From the terrace of the home we had recently moved into, we could see the large livestock fairgrounds built especially to accommodate sellers and buyers of livestock and other agricultural products from many towns and villages around our town. Most of the producers were Tunisian peasants. The buyers were Arab, Italian, Maltese, Spanish, and Jewish merchants.

During the war, the fairgrounds had been used by the Americans to store ammunitions. I remember the day when the entire town was shaking, as a huge explosion blasted the entire area.

Eventually the fairgrounds were restored to their original purpose.

One day, I was about eleven or twelve years old, I witnessed how French soldiers encircled the fairgrounds, which we called the *Rohba*. There were doctors and military law enforcement agents with them. They checked every male Tunisian peasant who was present as a buyer or as a seller and gave them a quick "medical checkup" in order to determine if they were fit for the army. Basically they just touched their arms to see if they had strength in their muscles. Afterwards they put the men into army trucks and drove away, leaving behind their wives, their children, their parents and their products, including their livestock, without any concern for what would become of them.

Shortly thereafter, a friend of my father's, who was an important figure at the courthouse, asked my father if I could help the poor peasant women and relatives and listen to their grievances in order to communicate with the French military authority, as they did not know any French at all, while I was fluent in both Arabic and French.

After talking with me, my father accepted to let me do the work as a volunteer in this project. My father's friend made the necessary arrangements and put at my disposal a room with a desk and chairs at the court building in order to receive the peasants every Thursday, as we had no school on that day. They came to me to complain and to try to alleviate their suffering by corresponding with army authorities in order to find their loved ones. I wrote so many letters to the army that I eventually found the trace of the men in question.

Every Thursday I stayed late to help the poor people with their complaints. Everyone came from far away and was sometimes without any means of communication. I listened patiently to

*Old city, Rue du Contrôle Civil
Justice de Paix is on the right and below. The courthouse where the author helped poor families.*

their grievances, but sometimes they repeated the same thing again and again. I was taking notes from what they were saying in Bedouin Arabic. They tried to dictate to me their message. Here are some of the words they were using in Bedouin Arabic:

Belahy A'alik Goloo Melly Hazoohoo El Aasker Wana Nebki Alih. Rani Tooaheshtoo Ktir Ektir, Oogalbi Mejrooah Wayneiya Hmor Menooah, Goloo Houa Rohy Oogalbi.

Translation in English of this typical complaint:

Tell him for God's sake, since the French soldiers took him in their truck I did not stop crying for him. I miss him a lot and my heart is aching and my eyes are red from crying. Tell him he is my heart and my soul.

I was happy to do this kind of work and to be able to help, as I knew the meaning of war and the suffering related to it. I could not understand why the French army didn't care to alleviate the burden of these poor Bedouin families, who were honest people without any malice.

DESTINY

Forge your destiny as long as you can run
Until your dreams dissipate in the sun.
Save your dignity and look for insight
As this is your own source of light.

Your knowledge will not fade away
As long as you stay active day-by-day.
You are what you want and what you can be
Take my word for it and you will see.

Shaping your life should be your endeavor
As it may retain some qualities forever.
Life, the ultimate reality, is anchored in you
But those who unveil it are rare and few.

What you read and experience is meant for you
Don't look at what others understand and do.
They have a totally different destiny
  and affinity
What may guide you
  counts on your own ability.

FEELINGS

During our childhood
  some feelings we sensed
Without knowing the reason
  and we commenced
To try understanding.
  We soon realized that we don't
Nevertheless, we enjoyed them,
  even if we won't.

When we encounter something
  completely new,
Sometimes we realize
  that much escapes our view,
As without seeing the wind,
  we feel the breeze
Without seeing earth's gravity,
  we walk with ease.

Some people are born
  with a more accurate sight,
But they cannot see what's
  in a drop of blood inside.

CHILDHOOD REGAINED

They need a microscope to show them
 more detail
But it's just an appearance;
 the essence is to no avail.

With the help of technology
 we will soon discover
Our planet's treasures,
 our own remain under cover,
Deep within ourselves,
 waiting for our yearning
To show us how to happiness
 we could be turning.

WHICH WAY TO GO

The first time we opened our eyes
We were blinded by the sun's rays;
We did not know what we wanted,
But we took everything for granted.

No one knew that this light is temporary
We couldn't ask anyone contemporary.
As no one could tell us or be our guide,
Essential questions remained on the side.

We take life as we see it,
   without explanation,
Everyone left alone to act
   upon his inclination
Many people are pretending
   to know more,
Showing others the
   "way to heaven's door".

Who would know?
   Even smart ones pretend too.
Let them believe that they know a thing or two.

CHILDHOOD REGAINED

The truth is, there are questions
  we do not ask.
We eat and sleep and
  try to do our daily task.

Many think about what happens
  after this life,
But no one asks any question,
  even to his wife.
As long as there is food, pleasure,
  and so-called gain,
The sun is still here
  to give us strength and lift our pain

Man's choice is to ignore
  himself and listen to the dark,
Or, deep inside, stay calm
  until he finds his own spark.
Only then can he decide
  which way to go, alone:
Listen to his fears or follow
  the light of his own.

SPIRITUAL LIFT

I was too young to understand
　or retain my parents' tales,
I just recall some fragments
　of these stories, not all details.
They help me take all the world
　has to offer like a gift.
In fact these stories silently
　give me a "spiritual lift".

Each of us carries within himself,
　since birth,
Seeds of goodness, love and spiritual
　worth,
As well as those of hatred,
　and unkindness,
Those of sound health and
　those of future illness;

Those of intelligence as well
　as those of stupidity.
It is up to us to choose which seeds
　should have validity,

Which ones we should develop and
   which ones to ignore
The results depend on our way
   of life and its core.

It is not always the "good"
   that makes us glad
And it is not always the "bad"
   which makes us sad.
The feelings that we sense
   with melancholy, with joy, and
With happiness make us discover
   where we really stand.

EMILE TUBIANA

THEIR MORAL VALUES

In the world in which we live,
Where we always take and give
We should aim to maintain stability
To the best of our skill and ability

It is understood that every one of us
May he be unknown or famous,
Toward his family has obligations
As toward society and his relations.

Parents couldn't learn as much as we,
But on certain things we must agree.
In us their moral values they instilled,
As our hearts with wisdom they filled.

Grandfather, father, besides their
  obligations,
Found time to tell their stories with
  patience.
I owe them so much, I will share with you
What I believe to be worthwhile and true.

HOPE

Times became rough,
But we had to be tough.
In order to cope,
We kept up faith and hope.
We needed to strive,
In order to survive.

THE GEM

They topple mountains,
   valleys they scour,
Searching for the gem
   with all their power.
They cross the seas and the rivers,
Their voyage only dust delivers.
They think they are big and smart,
The value of the moment they discard.
Happy those who in silence remain,
From touching embers they refrain.
The wise ones just stay home,
To find the treasure in their inner dome

GIFTS OF LIFE

A moment of life
Cannot be kept.
If we don't live it
Its loss we accept.

The time we sleep
Is definitely lost,
But gives us strength
For journey's length.

Natural beauty
Has its value in store,
Is self-sufficient,
Needs no décor.

Accept gifts of life,
They are not in vain,
Special for you,
Bringing only gain.

www.ingramcontent.com/pod-product-compliance
Lightning Source LLC
Chambersburg PA
CBHW051544010526
44118CB00022B/2571